- 0. JAN 1977

HOGG

6379530

394.0942   4/7

D1582118

HERTFORD

This book is due for return on or before the date shown. You
may extend its loan by bringing the book to the library

Please renew/return this item by the last date shown.

So that your telephone call is charged at local rate,
please call the numbers as set out below:

	From Area codes 01923 or 0208:	From the rest of Herts:
Renewals:	01923 471373	01438 737373
Enquiries:	01923 471333	01438 737333
Minicom:	01923 471599	01438 737599

L32b

TEL 54965 TELEX 81512

17 NOV 1979

20 JUL 1990

28 AUG 1991

12 DEC 2002

LOAN

30 MAY 1992

26 JUN 1992

- 9 FEB 2008

8|12

17 JUL 1992

14 AUG 1992

12 MAR 2002

29 SEP 2007

L 33

CUSTOMS AND
TRADITIONS
OF ENGLAND

Books by the same author:

Odd Aspects of England

Castles of England

A Guide to English Country Houses

Inns and Villages of England

A Second Book of Inns and Villages of England

Malta: Blue-Water Island

Exploring Britain with SHELL

etc

CUSTOMS AND TRADITIONS OF ENGLAND

Garry Hogg

David & Charles : Newton Abbot

Bishops Stortford Library
The Causeway, Bishops Stortford
Herts. CM23 2EJ
Telephone: 54946

HERTFORDSHIRE
COUNTY LIBRARY
394.0942
6379530

ISBN 0 7153 5373 X

COPYRIGHT NOTICE

© GARRY HOGG 1971

All rights reserved. No part of this publication
may be reproduced, stored in a retrieval system,
or transmitted, in any form or by any means,
electronic, mechanical, photocopying, recording
or otherwise, without the prior permission of
David & Charles (Publishers) Limited

Set in twelve on thirteen point Plantin
and printed in Great Britain by
W J Holman Limited Dawlish
for David & Charles (Publishers) Limited
South Devon House   Newton Abbot   Devon

CONTENTS

ACKNOWLEDGEMENTS

I should like to thank the following for permission to use the photographs reproduced in this book :

The British Tourist Authority, plates on pages 11, 13, 19, 27, 43, 59, 61, 63, 65, 67, 71, 95, 99, 101, 105
R. D. Barrett-Lennard, 15, 17, 23
'Knutsford Guardian', 21
Dempster's Studio, 25
British Travel Association, 29, 35, 69, 73, 81, 91, 107
Sheffield Newspapers Ltd, 31
Raymonds News Agency, 33
Western Times Co Ltd, 37, 39
Harvey Green, 41
Gloucestershire Newspapers Ltd, 45
'Evening Post', Bristol, 47
'Hampshire Chronicle', 49
'Kent Messenger', 51
'Lancashire Evening Post', 53
Brownlow, Nottingham, 55
'Scunthorpe Evening Telegraph', 57
'Oxford Mail & Times', 75
Reece Winstone, Bristol, 77
D. J. Wheadon, Chard, 79
J. Walker, 83
J. Wood, Rye, 85
'Sussex Life', 87
Hastings Corporation, 89
Herald Photographic Services, 93
Sanderson & Dixon Ltd, 97
Nellie Felton, Leeds, 103

FOREWORD

It would seem desirable to establish right away just what is meant by the terms customs and traditions, as used in the context of this book, for they are terms that carry more than one interpretation. It is, for example, the custom to pass the port round the table at formal dinners in one direction rather than the other; for audiences to rise to their feet when the National Anthem is played; for families with children to migrate to the seaside when the summer holidays begin. It is a tradition that men armed with shot-guns resort to the moors and elsewhere, on specific dates and thereafter, to slaughter inoffensive partridge, pheasant and grouse; that flags should be flown at half-mast on the death of royalty or other notable personages; that loyal supporters of Oxford and Cambridge should sport the appropriate favours on the annual Boat Race Day. But neither custom nor tradition (and the terms are virtually interchangeable here), in that guise, is the subject of the pages that follow, interesting as they might prove to be if they were researched in depth.

In these pages, customs and traditions are considered, essentially, as manifestations of impulses felt deeply, even if only subconsciously or indeed quite unconsciously, by those who take part in them. Many—perhaps the majority—of those described and illustrated in detail in this book have origins that are wholly lost in 'the dark backward and abysm of time'. In many cases it is possible only to hazard an uncertain guess as to why such-and-such custom or tradition first had its being, and why it should have survived throughout the evolving ages that have brought it, surprisingly, into this latter half of the twentieth century; changed, may be, in some details but fundamentally much as it was when it first appeared, several hundreds, even a thousand and more years ago.

It is a rash individual who will state categorically the line by which superstition and religion are demarcated. It is probably no more than the truth to state that the most interesting, and the most flourishing, of our customs and traditions are those that have their roots deep down in the soil of superstition tilled by our remotest ancestors. The Church may have striven, first to destroy both the manifestation and the impulse that gave birth to it, and then, sensing defeat, to channel it into more acceptable ways; but many of these customs and traditions have withstood every form of impact, whether overt and forceful or merely that of apathy and the flow of sophistication. Thus, many of them have survived until today; and not a few of these bid fair to survive into the foreseeable future.

The curious may speculate as to why so many subjects that seem obvious candidates for inclusion in this book should have been omitted from it. Why, they may ask, are we not given, for example, the University Boat Race that has been rowed for so many decades? What about The Derby? The Grand National? The Cup Final at Wembley? The Test Matches at Lords and the Oval and on other famous cricket grounds? Surely they are as essential threads in the warp and woof of life today as any that have won a place in these arbitrary pages?

It is difficult to answer without giving offence—save by reiterating that the great majority of the customs and traditions recorded here have an element in their composition that relates them more fundamentally to our way of life as it has evolved over the years, than those notable sporting occasions can possibly possess. There is, let us say, the 'smell of antiquity' about them; or, to change the metaphor, something of a patina, the result of persistent handling, down the years, that has given to the intangible a local habitation and a name.

No claim is put forward that the survey in these pages is a definitive one; or that the customs and traditions represented here are necessarily of greater interest and significance than all the others. To a large extent this is a personal selection. The examples chosen (out of so many) are those that, for one reason or another, appealed to the compiler over and above the alternatives available. The four dozen dealt with here in some detail are followed by a list of a hundred or so more that all deserve fuller treatment.

It should be borne in mind that, in spite of their apparent sturdy growth, some of these traditions are doomed to die—possibly even while this book is printing; others, hitherto annuals, may become triennials, even septennials. On the other hand, some that have wilted, or even died, may well be revived, thanks to the enthusiasm of local traditionalists unwilling to see the last of something inherently interesting and potentially capable of being resuscitated. There are, indeed, examples of customs and traditions that have been dead these many years —killed off, perhaps, by two world wars—but which have staged a miraculous revival and now flourish as they did when they first manifested themselves some hundreds of years ago. The English are, essentially, traditionalists; that being so, there is hope that the majority of these customs and traditions may survive into the twenty-first century and—who knows?—perhaps long after that.

G.H.

Groombridge, Sussex

MAY DAY MAYPOLE DANCING
ON ICKWELL GREEN
(3 miles west of Biggleswade)

The ancient custom of erecting a maypole on May Day and then danc-ing round it, once prevalent throughout the country, including London and other cities, has largely lapsed. It survives here and there, notably at Barwick-in-Elmet, Yorkshire; Welford-on-Avon, Warwickshire; Paganhill, Gloucestershire; Kingsteignton, Devonshire; and perhaps most notably at Ickwell Green in Bedfordshire. Here the ceremony, usually on the last Saturday in May though called 'May Day', is among the most colourful and elaborate in the whole country. It includes, as is the case in some other places, the ceremonial crowning of a girl from the village as Queen of the May.

Ickwell's 70ft spirally painted maypole is furnished with a large num-ber of coloured streamers. Their ends are held by children of the village, the girls attired in long, old-fashioned dresses, the boys in smocks, who dance round the maypole, treading a complicated series of steps which cause the streamers to interweave with one another and so form an intricate pattern in the air above their heads. While they tread this elaborate pattern of step and twist, the village green is further en-livened by a feature peculiar to the Ickwell ceremony : the presence of two 'Moggies', traditional figures whose origin is unknown. They have blackened faces and wear a weirdly designed garb, and each wields a besom—an old-fashioned type of broom consisting of a bundle of twigs fastened to a stick—with which to cajole spectators into contributing funds for the collecting-box they carry. In former times the Moggies commenced their activities on the evening prior to the actual ceremony at the maypole, when they distributed small bundles of twigs, sang their traditional Day Song, and left with a promise to return next day for payment in money or in kind according to the resources of the individ-ual householder. 'Moggie' is still a colloquial name for a kitten but it is hard to see any connection between kittens and these two men.

The crowning of the May Queen is at once a serious occasion and an excuse for revelry, and dates back at least to Tudor times. In the fourteenth century it might well be attended, in a town, by royalty; there was no *lèse majesté* in the election of the 'fairest maid of the village' in the presence of the reigning king and queen of the land, though the May Queen's reign would of course last only for twelve months.

HOCK-TIDE TUTTI-MEN, HUNGERFORD

Hock-tide (the second Tuesday after Easter) and Michaelmas Day have for centuries been regarded as the chief rent days of the year; the Tutti-men (or tithe-men) were the rent collectors. The picturesque and elaborate annual ceremony in this small country town adheres very closely to the one instituted way back in feudal times.

Hungerford is 'governed', not by mayor and corporation but by an elected Constable, a Portreeve, a Bailiff, and a Court of twelve Feoffees, or trustees. These are responsible for settling differences and administering the grazing, fishing and other local rights of the commoners. Annually therefore, on this Tuesday, at 8 o'clock in the morning, the Town Crier, using a seventeenth-century horn, a replica of the fourteenth-century horn presented to the town by John o' Gaunt when he granted the townsfolk fishing rights in the River Kennet, summons the commoners to the Court Leet. Here the officers for the following year are elected. Among these are two Tutti-men. Dressed in morning attire and top hat, and each bearing his staff of office, consisting of a rod adorned with ribbons and a bouquet topped by an orange, they set out on their rounds accompanied by the Orange Man, or Scrambler, who wears a cock-pheasant's tail-feathers in the silk hat which tops his morning dress. The Tutti-men are entitled to demand a coin from every man and a kiss from every woman. There is little chance of escape for the women for the Tutti-men are equipped with a light ladder and are entitled to enter any house by an upstairs window if the door is barred. An orange is exchanged for every kiss received: hence the attendance of the Orange Man.

The rounds completed, the remaining oranges and some of the coins are distributed among the children. Then the civic lunch is held, presided over by the newly elected Constable. There follows the ceremony of Shoeing the Colt, at which two farriers 'shoe' the soles of random visitors and commoners. Those who resist shoeing can be fined; those who submit eventually cry 'Punch!' and pay a small fee towards another round of that ever-popular drink. Drink, of course, flows freely; but the uninhibited revelry and violence that formerly attended Hock-tide festivals here and elsewhere, and were so strongly condemned by the church, are no longer a feature.

FENNY POPPERS, FENNY STRATFORD
(On A5, 45 miles north-west of London)

This straggling township might seem at first sight to have little to commend it. The first part of its name implies the sort of region in which it lies; the 'ford' indicates that the sluggish stream producing the marshy surroundings was once crossed here without a bridge; the 'Strat', as always, signifies a Roman origin: it lies astride Watling Street, the Roman through-way north-westwards from London. For decades past, until such traffic was largely drawn away from it by the construction of the M6 motorway, it had to endure the continuous thunder of heavy lorries roaring through its 'strait' single street. Its two old posting inns, the Cock, and the Bull, are still there to remind us of more leisurely days when the street knew only the traffic of stage coaches and horse-drawn waggons, interspersed from time to time by the activities of highwaymen temporarily deserting the more profitable Great North Road. It is believed, though the legend is not easy to substantiate, that these two inns provide the origin of the derogatory colloquial phrase: a cock-and-bull story.

From the eighteenth century, the heyday of the highwayman, comes another tradition, peculiar to the town: the ceremonial firing of the 'Fenny Poppers'. It takes place on 11 November, St Martin's Day and the patronal day therefore of St Martin's church, built by the antiquary Dr Browne. He presented to his church six miniature cannon. They are kept on a shelf in the tower, securely padlocked, and look more like mis-shapen pewter mugs than firearms. But on his birthday, St Martin's Day, every year they are taken down, charged with gunpowder, and fired at four-hourly intervals from 8 o'clock in the morning until 8 o'clock in the evening.

Though so small—perhaps 7in in height—they are so massively constructed that they weigh something like 20lb apiece. And since in the four salvoes they are required to use 'a guinea's-worth of gunpowder', which must be used up exactly in the final salvo, they produce a remarkably powerful explosion. The ceremony ends on a different note. After the final salvo, a special sermon is preached in the church, also under Dr Browne's bequest. And finally—more to the participants' taste, no doubt—a specially endowed supper is enjoyed by all.

Buckinghamshire

MAYORAL WEIGH-IN, HIGH WYCOMBE
(On A40, 25 miles north-west of London)

This annual ceremony is a relatively new one, compared with those dating back to the Middle Ages and earlier. Though local traditionalists claim that it dates back to the first Elizabeth, who commented on the generous proportions of the town's officials and implied that they were not working hard enough, in fact the earliest record of the ceremony is in 1893, when the newly elected mayor tipped the scales at a few pounds under 19 stone. (He was surpassed by a mayor in the late 'fifties who weighed almost 20 stone!) However, the procedure is designed to show whether the outgoing mayor has gained or lost weight during his year's term of office.

Mayoral Weighing Day is the first Monday after the middle of the month of May. On that day, the newly elected mayor and mayoress, the outgoing mayor and mayoress, the recorder, town clerk, aldermen and councillors, in order of seniority, present themselves in front of the town hall, where a massive set of scales has been erected. The Chief Inspector of Weights and Measures officiates. The outgoing mayor takes his seat in the pan beneath the recording dial. The inspector establishes his weight, and checks it against the record of the previous occasion, then communicates the result to the Beadle. Crying 'Oyez! Oyez!! Oyez!!!', the Beadle rings his bell for silence, and then announces the change in weight (if any). He cries 'Twelve stone, eight pounds' (or whatever it may be), capping this with 'And **some** more', if the outgoing mayor has gained weight; or capping it with 'And **no** more', if he has in fact lost weight. The exact gain or loss is not given, but there is heavy emphasis on the 'some' or the 'no' in his declaration. The implication of course is that a gain in weight argues a lack of diligence in office; a loss in weight argues self-sacrifice willingly undergone for the benefit and welfare of the townsfolk.

It is interesting to note that in 1951 this mayoral weighing ceremony was adopted by the town of Minneapolis in the United States. High Wycombe visitors to that town might however be surprised at some of the embellishments that have been devised there and the romantic additions that have been grafted on to the basic procedure. The 'Olde Englyshe' wording takes on a new character when delivered in Minneapolis.

16

Buckinghamshire

PANCAKE-DAY RACE AT OLNEY
(12 miles south-east of Northampton)

The great majority of traditional ceremonies are enacted by men only, or children. This, a rare and distinctive exception, is exclusively for women. They must all be established residents, not less than sixteen years of age, and must conform to the hard-and-fast rules of the race, which was almost certainly instituted as long ago as 1445. Each competitor must wear a skirt (jeans are banned) with an apron over it, and a scarf on her head. She must carry a hot frying-pan in her hand, with a pancake in it ready for tossing, fresh from her own kitchen stove.

At 11.30 on the morning of Shrove Tuesday, the day before Ash Wednesday and the beginning of the traditional Lenten Fast, the bell-ringer warns competitors to be ready. At 11.45 the People's Warden, usually wearing antiquated garb, gives the signal for the race to commence by ringing the old Town Crier's bell. The race is over a course nearly a ¼ mile in length, beginning at the village inn and ending at the church porch. Immediately on starting the race each competitor must toss her pancake, and catch it. It is tossed a second time on approaching the church and a third time at the church porch. The first competitor to arrive, with her tossed pancake still in her pan, is acclaimed the winner, a coveted title held for the next twelve months. She receives a kiss from the vicar, together with a prayer book as prize. The other competitors have to be content with a kiss apiece from the bellringer, who receives a tossed pancake from each in exchange for the kiss.

The origin of the race is believed to be that an Olney housewife, seeking to use up her butter and eggs before Lent, was interrupted by the shriving-bell calling all to receive absolution, and ran to church with frying-pan and batter in hand. The bell is known locally as the Pancake Bell for this reason. It is interesting to note that twenty years or so ago the township of Liberal in Kansas, USA, challenged the villagers of Olney to a race under the same conditions. The Olney housewives won, perhaps because they had had 500 years' practice This has happily led to the institution of a pancake race as an annual event on both sides of the Atlantic.

ROYAL MAY DAY FESTIVAL, KNUTSFORD

This century-old ceremony is among the most spectacular of all the May Day festivals, and acquired its unique 'Royal' because it was patronised by the Prince of Wales later to become Edward VII. The small town is the 'Cranford' of Mrs Gaskell's novel, and traditionally derived its name from the crossing of a ford there by King Canute nearly a thousand years ago. His legendary gesture of sprinkling sand in front of a bridal party and wishing them as many children as there were grains of sand is the origin of the unique Knutsford tradition of 'sanding' the streets for weddings: patterns and mottoes in white sand on dark. These are to be seen on Royal Festival Day, the Saturday nearest to May Day.

An ambitious procession, a small-scale version of London's Lord Mayor's Show, forms up outside the Town Hall at 2 o'clock, to make its leisurely way to The Heath, on the town's edge, the scene of its climax. It varies annually in composition, but is always led by the Town Crier and Marshal. There follow troupes of country dancers, silver prize bands, royal jesters, characters from the Robin Hood legends, a genuine sedan chair of the 'Cranford' era, floats portraying a wide variety of themes, a succession of landaus conveying court ladies and maids of honour, escorted by Beefeaters and foot guards, and eventually the state coach, loaned by the Lord Mayor of Liverpool, conveying the newly elected queen to her throne on The Heath, where she will be ceremonially crowned by the current Crown Bearer. Queen, crown bearer, maids of honour and all court officials must be children resident in Knutsford; the queen not older than fourteen, her maids of honour not older than ten, though the crown bearer is by tradition a year or two older than the queen. The crown, unusually for such ceremonies, is retained permanently by each new queen, a unique and cherished memento.

It is impossible to describe in a few paragraphs the extraordinary richness and variety of this annual festival. The organisers vie with one another to outdo in originality and panache what they achieved only the year before. A pleasing feature of this occasion, in these sadly commercialised days, is that after all legitimate expenses have been met, the moneys received are allocated to various local charities and 'the benefit of the inhabitants of the Township of Knutsford'.

THE FURRY DANCE, HELSTON
(On A394, 13 miles east of Penzance)

The word 'Furry' (too often mistakenly replaced by 'Floral') is a Cornish corruption either of the Romans' *feria,* a festival, or of the Celtic *feur,* a holiday. The festival takes place annually on 8 May, the day sacred to the 'quaint old Cornish town's' patron, St Michael, but it dates back well before Christianity, to the age when Celtic rites of 'fetching the summer home' at the end of winter were practised. Probably because there is so much decoration with flowers and branches, the Victorians dubbed it 'Floral', which in their eyes safely removed from it any taint of paganism. Today, the hundreds who lightheartedly take part in the celebrations doubtless think of it only as an annual excuse for large-scale merrymaking.

And large-scale it certainly is! Early in the morning the younger folk collect flowers and branches, especially of beech and sycamore, to decorate their town. Then they dance through its narrow streets, singing the traditional 'Hal-an-Tow' song. At noon, the mayor, in full mayoral regalia, heads the people in the principal dancing of the day, the 'Invitation Dance'. Men wear morning dress and top hats, women their finery and flowing head-dress. Throughout the bunting-decked streets the couples go, the leading couples being by tradition Helston-born and wearing lilies-of-the-valley in their buttonholes. They dance through the open doors of houses and shops alike, bringing 'Good Luck' to their occupants before dancing out of the back doors; if a door should be closed to them, they knock on it till it is opened. At intervals the couples bow and curtsey to one another; in this way they are 'bringing summer' to one another personally and publicly. Throughout the long day the numbers of dancing couples swell as more and more visitors pour into Helston, to fall in with the little town's spirit of uninhibited gaiety and good humour.

Over the years, of course, legends have grown up around the place. One of these is to the effect that in remote times their patron St Michael was challenged by the Devil for the ownership of the town and its inhabitants. Discomfited, the Devil hurled a block of local granite as he took flight; it may be seen (they will tell you) embedded in the wall of an inn; and from this 'Hell Stone' comes the name, Helston!

MARHAMCHURCH REVEL, MARHAMCHURCH
(Off A39, 3 miles south-east of Bude)

Christianity reached Cornwall centuries before Augustine 'brought the Christian Faith to Canterbury' in AD597. A hundred years earlier, Marwenne, daughter of the Christian King Brychan of Brecknock, established a hermitage here and the village grew around this; today's fifteenth-century church is the most recent dedicated to her. St Marwenne's Feast Day is 12 August, and from the Middle Ages onwards Revel Sunday has been the Sunday following, its associated secular revel taking place on the Monday. It is so to this day; Cornish feeling for tradition being so strong, it should survive.

The Queen of the Revel is its central figure. She must have been born in Marhamchurch and attended the local school; she must have been elected by the sixty or so children of the village, half-a-dozen of whom become her attendants. Over her traditional white dress she wears a blue cloak, handed down from queen to queen. Her herald and page wear historic costume. After robing, they pass in procession to the reputed site of St Marwenne's cell, near the war memorial. There the queen is officially crowned by Father Time, in flowing robe, with scythe and hour-glass: 'Now look!', he intones, 'That this by all be seen, I here do crown thee, of this year, the Queen'.

Riding a white horse led by a farmer in smock and top hat, preceded by a town band and followed by the children in fancy dress, she now makes a ceremonial circuit of the village, before reaching Revel Field, close to the church, where she declares the Marhamchurch Revel open. Then the entertainment really begins. There is Cornish wrestling, country dancing, maypole dancing, judging of fancy dresses, gymnastic displays, trials of strength, individual competitions for men and for women. The last event is the traditional pram race, a hilarious affair, which culminates in dancing and refreshments, the awarding of the many prizes and a closing ceremony. Many anonymous donations have been received by the sponsors. When expenses have been paid, and the Parish Church and Methodist Chapels received their due, the remainder is distributed among the many local deserving charities. Though Marhamchurch is no more than a spot on a map, it has a healthy life and tradition of its own and, for all its remoteness, flourishes today as it has done for so many centuries.

Cornwall (and Devonshire)

MIDSUMMER EVE BONFIRES

November 5th, 'Guy Fawkes Night', is by no means the only night when bonfires are lit. Midsummer Eve is an infinitely older 'date', celebrated in pre-Christian times by the lighting of great fires and widespread animal (and sometimes human) sacrifice. Though the Church tried hard, it never succeeded in stamping-out the basic rites, whose origins of course lay in pagan sun-worship, though it modified them and even turned some of them to its own advantage. But bonfire-lighting, and the ignition of tar-filled wooden barrels and hurling them about, remain a traditional Midsummer Eve ceremony to this day, notably in the Westcountry, particularly in Cornwall but also in neighbouring Devonshire, for instance in Ottery St Mary (opposite).

Bonfires are lit along the hilltops in a chain that stretches eastwards from St Ives (where the bonfire may actually be lit by the mayor himself), transforming them one after another into lofty flaming torches for all to see. Many of them are also focal points for the re-enacting of traditional rites. Flowers and herbs may be thrown into the flames by The Lady of the Flowers, to an ancient but meaningful incantation. Young couples, even in our sophisticated age, sometimes leap together across the flames (a visual echo of the former sacrifice) to ensure for themselves fertility and prosperity. The warm ashes from the dying bonfires are sometimes gathered up and taken home 'for luck', to be retained until next Midsummer Eve, when they will be duly replaced by ashes from the succeeding bonfire.

Smaller, 'mobile' bonfires, too, are a feature of this Midsummer Eve revelry. Old wooden barrels are filled with scraps of canvas, kindling, shavings and any other readily combustible material that lies to hand. Tar is poured over the contents, and the barrels themselves, and then the youths of the district vie with one another in demonstrating how long they can hold the flaming barrels above their heads and how far and accurately they can hurl them, flaming as they go. This is dangerous play, and efforts are made year after year to put an end to it. But the tradition is more deep-rooted than either participants or authorities perhaps realise; behind all this, unknown to them, lurks the pagan god, Baal himself.

Cornwall

PADSTOW HOBBY-HORSE

Two lines of the song traditionally chanted by the Padstow merry-makers suggest that this May Day ceremony is pagan in origin. 'Unite and unite, let us unite, For summer is a-cummin in!' they sing; those first lines of doggerel verse are heard outside the Golden Lion inn immediately after the last stroke of midnight on 30 April: now truly it is May; summer has come. There is the underlying motif of seasonal and welcome change. This little township at the mouth of the Camel estuary is gaily decked for the occasion; the ships lying in the harbour, big and little, are dressed overall.

The mainspring of the day's festivities is the hobby-horse. He is a grotesque monster: a Padstow man encased in a boat-shaped structure of shiny black material tightly stretched over a hoop frame encircling him, below which, through a mini-skirt of black, his white-clad legs protrude. He wears a fantastic head-dress that has something in common with an aborigine's mask, with garish coloured stripes and a fearsome display of fang-like teeth that, in less sophisticated days, struck terror into the hearts of all beholders. He dances furiously through the narrow streets, preceded by a white-clad, clown-like figure brandishing a menacing club and known as the Teaser. There may also be other attendants with blackened faces, to whip up the procession. Another hint that the ceremony is of pagan origin is to be found in the fact that every now and then some young woman will be whipped beneath the hobby horse's skirt and have her face blacked. This is held to be a suitably emasculated form of an ancient fertility rite designed to ensure the woman a husband and offspring.

The procession calls at various houses, urging the menfolk to 'leave the bride that lies by your side' because it is 'now the merry morning of May'. Alms are begged for at the houses of the more affluent citizens. The local band works up the excitement and everyone dances madly in the streets. Then follows the traditional 'death' of the hobby-horse; the violent music softens, the motion fades, the hobby-horse sinks to the ground as though expiring. But at a crashing thump from the drummer he revives, the music swells to a new crescendo, the hobby-horse leaps into action again and the triumphant refrain is repeated yet once more: 'Summer is a-cum today!'

28

PLAGUE SUNDAY AT EYAM
(Off A623, 5 miles north of Bakewell)

This annual service, held on the last Sunday in August, is not as macabre as its name would suggest, for it is a service of rejoicing and thanksgiving. It springs from the disaster that hit England in 1665, when the Great Plague swept through the country, decimating its population until the Great Fire of London swept all clean.

The plague germ reached the village of Eyam, 800ft up on the moors, in a parcel of clothing delivered to the occupant of what is now universally known as Plague Cottage, adjoining the ancient church. There were fewer than 400 inhabitants, then; within months more than 250 of them had died: the plague had taken hold. Rector William Mompesson called on the villagers to isolate themselves: no man, woman or child, on oath, was to leave the village, so that contagion might be checked, and neighbouring villagers spared. Every single one agreed. Food was brought from outlying villages and farms, and from the great house of the Duke of Devonshire, Chatsworth. It was set down on a wide stone over which a spring of clear water flowed, at a safe distance from Eyam. This became known as Mompesson's Well. Not far away there is a dell, locally known as Cucklett Delf. Here Mompesson, having closed his church as a precaution against the spread of the plague, held services throughout the thirteen months of the self-imposed isolation of his flock.

And here, each year, Plague Sunday service is held, to commemorate the ordeal of the Eyam folk, whose self-sacrifice was justified as there were no further outbreaks of plague in the county. A brass band heads a long procession from the church, along the lane between the drystone walls, to Cucklett Delf. All Eyam's inhabitants are there; and visitors from far and wide, drawn by curiosity and by admiration for that fine gesture of three centuries ago. The lane opens out into the horseshoe of the dell that is enclosed by trees and shrubs. Then a simple commemorative service is held. There is an address appropriate to the occasion. There are special prayers of intercession for the hundreds who died in agony during the plague, and who are remembered almost as if it had all happened but yesterday. And a specially composed Plague Hymn is sung by the surpliced choir boys and men from Eyam's church, in whose graveyard you may see so many tombs of those who died in the village 300 years ago.

Derbyshire

SHROVE-TIDE FOOTBALL, ASHBOURNE
(On A515)

Whereas almost all of the traditional ceremonies have become emasculated over the centuries and happily lost the uninhibited boisterousness, even violence, by which so many of them were accompanied, this certainly cannot be said of some of the Shrove-tide 'games' still held in various parts of the country, and most notably in this small market town near the beauty spots of the Derbyshire Dales on the southern edge of the Peak District. At Ashbourne, players are tough and determined, prepared to struggle equally on land and in very cold water at this time of the year, to play their part and survive intact the rough-and-tumble of a traditional contest.

At 2 o'clock on Shrove Tuesday the heavy (and soon to be water-logged) leather ball, painted white and embellished with the Union Jack or some emblem associated with the 'personality' (it has sometimes been royalty) who will be starting the game, is let loose near the centre of the town. From that moment onwards until midnight, and sometimes well into Ash Wednesday, it is 'in play'. The players, an unlimited number, are divided into 'Uppards' and 'Downards', according to whether they were born above or below Henmore Brook, which flows through the lower part of the town. Their aim is to convey (by fair means or foul: it maters not!) the ball to one or other of two goals, mill-wheels at Clifton and Sturston, 3 miles apart. When a goal has been scored the scorer claims the ball as his trophy, and a new one is thrown into play.

There are no rules, written or observed, save that a goal must be scored by a legitimate Downard or Uppard; there is virtually no time-limit; there is no specific field of play, so shop-keepers wisely barricade their windows and householders do likewise. Streets become battle-fields in no time; the players are no respecters of property; the police tend to turn a blind eye, within limits! The true focus of play usually seems to be the shallow brook running between muddy banks beneath overhanging trees. Here the toghest aspects of play—'fight' is the more appropriate term—can be witnessed, though mere spectators run the risk of becoming unwittingly involved, to their peril and very real risk of injury in the melee. Perhaps, here, 'ceremony' is a misnomer; the occasion is a protracted test of communal endurance.

Derbyshire

WELL-DRESSING
(Villages lie to the east of the A515 Ashbourne-Buxton road)

The tradition of dressing-the-well exists in various parts of England; it is most notably seen in a dozen or so Derbyshire villages such as Tissington, Barlow, Wirksworth, Youlgreave and Tideswell. This is a region of carboniferous limestone, where water supplies are notoriously unpredictable. Though well-dressing may date back to pagan times, for centuries past it has been an essentially religious ceremony, a form of pious thanksgiving to a merciful God for His gift of that most vital commodity.

The origin is thought to date back to the period of the Black Death which, in 1348, decimated the population of the country. Wells like those at Tissington remained pure, and people came great distances to obtain water from them; not one death from plague was recorded in the district. Alternatively it may date from 1615, when there was a twenty-week drought over the country, though these wells remained full.

The wells are dressed for Ascension Day each year. The villagers, from the oldest to the youngest, compete to make their well the most beautifully ornate of them all. (In Tissington there are five wells: Town Well, Hall Well, Yew Tree Well, Hands Well and Coffin Well.) Behind each well a large wooden frame is erected, and plastered smoothly with soft clay. Into the surface a profusion of natural substances—daisies, flower petals, fragments of the local quartz, fir-cones, pieces of moss, beans, birds' feathers, berries, and so forth—are pressed in such a way as to form a boldly and yet subtly 'painted' picture. The picture itself is usually surmounted by a biblical text or some traditional pious sentiment. There seems no limit to the craftsmanship and artistic ingenuity of the amateurs of each village; the aim is to make each a work of art more memorable than that of the year before.

The climax is reached on Ascension Day, the Thursday before Whitsuntide. At 11 o'clock in the morning a service is held in the village church—in the case of Tideswell in the 'Cathedral of the Peak'. After this there is a procession of clergy and congregation from each decorated well to the next in turn, to bless them. It is a mass expression of thanksgiving for the service rendered by them so generously so many years ago, and still rendered by them even in this modern industrial age.

BLESSED ARE
THE MERCIFUL

19 61

FOR THEY SHALL
OBTAIN MERCY

LAMMAS FAIR, HONITON (and elsewhere)
(On A30, 17 miles east of Exeter)

The word Lammas is the medieval form of the Anglo-Saxon Loaf Mass. This was a religious ceremony during which a loaf of bread made from flour derived from the first-ripened wheat of the season, together with a sheaf of that wheat, was consecrated. Though now a religious ceremony, it undoubtedly originated in pre-Christian times when seed-time and harvest were recurrent mysterious features of the community's life and vaguely associated in the communal mind with fertility rites and the worship of the life-giving sun. Inevitably it later came to be associated with the institution of the Harvest Festival, the older name for which was Festival of First Fruits.

Strictly, Lammas is celebrated on 1 August, or on the Sunday closest to that date; but over the years, in varying localities, the date has been advanced or retarded. The actual celebration of First Fruits seems to occur most widely in the South and the Westcountry, though Loaf Mass Day is an official Scottish Quarter Day.

For at least seven centuries in some places, the date has been the occasion for something more ambitious than the mere consecration of a loaf and a sheaf: an occasion for a market fair. The ancient symbol for this has always been the glove. It was a signal to merchants that they might come and trade in the town; it was a legal undertaking, established by Edward I, that soldiery would protect them from the bandits on the approaches to the town who were constantly on the watch for just such prey. The parading of the glove is the central feature of the fairs that survive. In Honiton the Town Crier, in cocked hat and gold-lace-trimmed scarlet garb, bears the gilded glove aloft on a garlanded pole, crying 'Oyez, Oyez! The Glove is Up! The Fair is Open! God Save the Queen!' The glove is placed above the porch of an inn. Then 'hot pennies' are thrown, to be scrambled for by children. The ritual is repeated from a second inn on the following day. The fair that is thus opened is mainly for pleasure, but, in the old tradition, there is still the buying and selling of ponies and cattle.

The date is the Tuesday before the third Wednesday in July. Exeter holds its Lammas Fair on the same day, with similar ceremony but no fair. Barnstaple, far to the north, parades the glove and holds its fair much later, in mid-September.

RAM FAIR, KINGSTEIGNTON
(On A380, 16 miles south of Exeter)

With its neighbouring villages, Bishopsteignton, Teingrace, Combein-teignhead and Stokeinteignhead, this small township takes its name from the river Teign, near whose estuary it is to be found. It is the scene of an annual fair, held every Whit Monday, the remote origins of which remain permanently in dispute. Antiquaries and others maintain that they date back to pagan times; not unnaturally, the Church, which has long had to accept the tradition, maintains that the annual occasion dates back only to the early days of Christianity in this country. Basic-ally, however, there is nothing to choose: quite certainly it is connected with the impulse of thanksgiving for the blessing of water, that always vital but often unpredictable commodity.

Kingsteignton is situated on a slope to the north of the estuary. Its inhabitants, at least until modern piped water came their way, have always depended on springs situated above the village (it is little more than that, even today), in an area still marked on large-scale maps as Well Head. At some remote time—pre-Christian or early Christian, for beliefs vary—the springs dried up. The pagans (if it was they) met to make sacrifice of a ram to their gods, before their crops withered and cattle died; the Christians (if it was they) assembled to pray for water for their community, not forgetting the importance of baptism. And—miraculously—water immediately began to flow once more; since then it has never once failed.

Happily for those of us who look back nostalgically on less sophisti-cated times, tradition dies hard. So, today the garnished carcass of a young ram is ceremonially paraded through the streets, decked with ribbons and flowers. Meanwhile sports, pony races, games and varied displays are in full swing; money has already been collected for prizes, but most people agree that the chief prizes are those that all may re-ceive: the slices of barbecued ram lamb distributed to all and sundry, as they always have been. There was a day when these valued slices cost a penny a time; the money so received went to the farmer or house-hold that had provided the animal. Pennies were worth more in those days, and certainly the man who had contributed the carcass made a substantial profit on that memorable Whit Monday!

GARLAND DAY, ABBOTSBURY
(On B3157, 8 miles south-west of Dorchester)

This hamlet of mellow stone and snug thatch, is one of the most pictur-esque in all Dorset, a county noted for the quiet beauty of its villages. On its outskirts are the remains of a Benedictine Abbey, from which it derives its name. These consist mainly of a fine gateway, and a magnifi-cent fifteenth-century tithe-barn, one of the noblest in England. It stands on an elevation above the village, overlooking the beautiful swannery which is unique in the country, and, just beyond that, the Chesil Bank, that extraordinary rampart of graduated pebbles that runs eastwards from Abbotsbury to Portland, some 12 miles along the coast. Between Chesil Bank and the mainland lie the dual waterways, East and West Fleet; it is this most unusual stretch of water that in the past made the village famous for its inshore fishing.

Only one family is fishing today but it loyally maintains the tradition of blessing the boats, even though there is only one boat left to bless. Formerly, wreaths and garlands were fashioned, paraded round the vil-lage and brought down to the water's edge, one for each boat; the blessing given, the boats put out to sea, where the garlands were thrown overboard to float on the water until they disintegrated into a mass of scattered flowers. The ceremony (of which variants are still to be seen at many places round the coast) is of very ancient origin; it is parallel to the sacrificial rites carried out to ensure fertility of crop and beast in the field. At Abbotsbury, boat and water and fishermen alike were blessed in this way.

Today the children make the garlands and, on or about 13 May, parade them on wooden frames so massive that two children must carry each; designs are traditional, handed down over the years by the fisher families of the village. The village of course is en fete; money is col-lected and shared out among the children. Today, though, the wreaths and garlands are laid at the foot of the village War Memorial, a change of routine that commenced when there were casualties among the fishermen themselves and the industry began to die. So what started in remote times as a pagan ceremony, and then became a purely local, semi-religious ceremony, has now almost lost its local significance and become largely irrelevant, though it remains so picturesque.

CHEESE-ROLLING, COOPER'S HILL
(4 miles east of Gloucester)

Cooper's Hill is a grassy slope near Birdlip Hill on the western scarp of the Cotswolds, dipping down a gradient of 1 in 3 towards the village of Brockworth. It has for at least 400 years been the scene, every Whit Monday, of a ceremony to commemorate the traditional right of local farmers and shepherds to graze their sheep on the common land of the district. Formerly, a maypole was erected on the top of the hill; latterly it has been a flagstaff. It marks the point of assembly at which the competitors meet annually to remind all and sundry of their forefathers' inalienable rights: the steep, turf-clad hill represents the common land. Only the young and strong and sure of foot take part in this dramatic downhill race; or rather, it should be called a downhill scramble, and it can be very dangerous indeed.

At exactly 6 o'clock in the evening the starting signal is given by the official starter who, by tradition, wears a livery consisting of an antique Cotswold shepherd's smock and a white 'beaver' hat. His task is to fire a pistol into the air and at the same time to release the rope behind which the scores of competitors have been held back, and to launch down the slope the cheese. This was originally a Double Gloucester, the cheese of the region; today it is customarily an imitation, protected by a stout wooden casing to prevent its disintegration as it leaps and bounces down the steep hill. The objective of the competitors is to overtake it before it has reached the bottom of the hill: an objective very rarely achieved, so swiftly and unpredictably does it leap down the hill in front of them.

The winner of the scramble, the first to reach the bottom, receives the cheese as a memento of his strength and skill; he receives also a small purse of money. He has certainly earned his reward for to race at that speed, shouldered by fellow-competitors all the way, calls for courage as well as fleetness and sureness of foot. Many competitors suffer damage to knees and ankles—if nothing worse. But even if they do not receive the prize, the acclamation of the hundreds who line the course is compensation; in the bright eyes of the girls of the district looking on they have won merit which will no doubt be individually rewarded later in the day.

CLIPPING CEREMONY, PAINSWICK
(On A46, 3 miles north of Stroud)

The word 'clipping' in this context has nothing to do with the annual trimming of the 100 magnificent yew trees that pattern the churchyard of this ancient church, the first of which were planted 200 years ago; though in fact they are quite often trimmed for this special occasion. Actually it is an old word for 'embracing', and refers here to the expression of pious devotion of the parishioners for their church. Similar ceremonies are held elsewhere: at Hastings in Sussex; Wirksworth and Burbage in Derbyshire; and Guiseley in Yorkshire. Nowhere, however, is it more picturesquely seen than among those centuries-old yew trees in the churchyard of St Mary's, Painswick, traditionally on the Sunday that falls nearest to 19 September.

First there is the procession, led by the band, that circles the churchyard. Then all the children of this small Cotswold town, dressed in their best and carrying garlands of flowers, join hands and surge towards the fine stone walls of the church, then retreat. They repeat this three times, singing as they do so the traditional Clipping Hymn, in which they are reinforced by the church choir and the hundreds of adult parishioners. The vicar then declares that their church has been duly 'clipped', and, standing on the stone steps at the corner of the tower, beneath the ornamental clock, he proceeds to deliver his special Clipping Sermon.

As is so often the case in ceremonies like this, which almost certainly had their origin in pre-Christian times though the church has long since adapted and modified them, the Clipping used to terminate in a wild scramble on the part of the older children and youths to the old vicarage, uttering as they ran the cry, 'High-Gates!'—a cry that remains unexplained to this day. Behaviour now is more decorous, but no self-respecting Painswick housewife would fail to produce the traditional round cake, topped by a splash of almond paste and having embedded within it a small china dog. It is known as Puppy Dog Pie. She may not realise this, but almost certainly in the remote past the dancing was round an improvised altar, on which was sacrificed some animal: an essential part of 'clipping' before this became associated with the church, and part of a ritual perhaps not fully understood even by the participants.

RUSH SUNDAY, BRISTOL

Centuries ago, rushes served as the normal 'carpet' in the homes of both rich and poor. Until comparatively recent times they were still used by the poorest cottage dwellers in those parts of England where rushes were easy to obtain. In some parts of the country, notably in the Lake District, the annual ceremony of bearing rushes, not to the cottages but to the church, as a token of gratitude for favours received, is still held, the pattern of the ceremony varying from one district to the next. Even today it may be witnessed, too, in one great city, Bristol.

In 1493, the year after Columbus unwittingly 'discovered' America, the then mayor of Bristol, one William Spenser, bequeathed a sum that would ensure the preaching of three sermons annually in Pentecost Week before his successors-in-office, in perpetuity. The only modification of the bequest that has been made in the 500 years since his day is that the number of sermons has been reduced to one, and this is invariably delivered on Whit Sunday. On that day, a procession of city dignitaries, led by the Lord Mayor preceded by the Sword Bearer (for Bristol is now a cathedral city), advances towards the thirteenth-to-fifteenth-century church of St Mary Redcliffe, one of the largest churches in all England. He is met and greeted there by the Lord Bishop of the diocese.

The procession continues on its way through the church's main door, and members take their allotted places. The church has been specially decorated for the occasion. Flowers are banked everywhere: it is almost as though it is Harvest Festival Sunday. To add to the floral effect, as many as possible of those attending the ceremony carry small bouquets or nosegays, a charming touch. But the most conspicuous feature, even if lowlier and less colourful than the flowers, is the rushes that have been strewn over the stone-slabbed floor of the huge nave. They have not been laid in any ornamental pattern; they have not been brought, as in some Lakeland villages, in bundles tied in colourful ribbons; nor have they been carried, as elsewhere, in the form of symbolic crosses or worked into the shape of floral harps or the legendary bulrush cradle of the infant Moses, as elsewhere again. Nevertheless, the simple strewing of the vast nave floor of this ancient church offers a beauty of simplicity and innocence which will linger long in the memory.

46

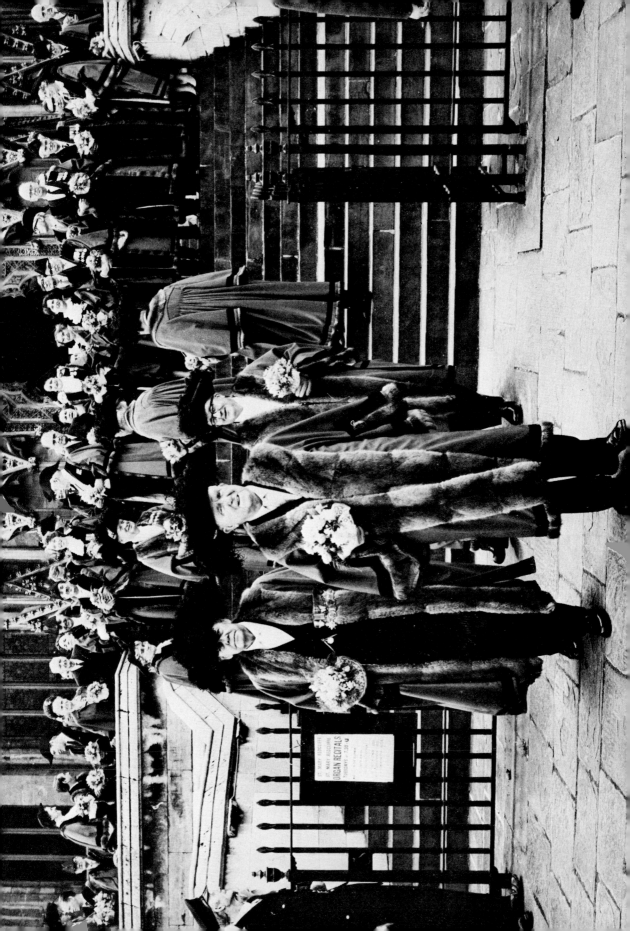

THE TICHBOURNE DOLE
(Off A31, 5 miles east of Winchester)

This may well be the most ancient 'dole' in the country, pre-dating even the Royal Maundy; it is certainly among the richest in tradition. The Tichbornes have been lords of the manor here for 800 years, and the dole springs from a gesture made by Lady Mabella, wife of one of the earliest in the line. On her death-bed she interceded with a harsh husband that he should have more regard for the welfare of the people on his estate. She urged him to set aside a piece of land to provide, in perpetuity, an annual dole of bread. He reluctantly agreed to spare just as much land as she, a dying woman, could encompass, torch in hand, before the flame died. The saintly woman crawled from her bed, took the torch he offered her, and miraculously succeeded in crawling round no less than 23 acres of land before both the torch flame and her own courageous life's flame were extinguished. The piece of land is known to this day as The Crawls. Before she died, she laid a curse: if any succeeding Tichborne broke faith with her request, then the line would become extinct.

The annual ceremony of distributing the Tichborne Dole is carried out on 25 March, Lady Day. In olden times the dole consisted of as many as 1,400 26oz loaves, with a purse containing two pence for those deserving applicants for whom no flour remained. Today, the traditional 30 hundredweight of flour is distributed by the head of the family, on the steps of Tichborne House, to approximately 200 villagers of Tichborne and neighbouring Cheriton. The distribution commences with a thanksgiving service in Latin, then the flour itself is blessed, in pious memory of its saintly donor. After this, it is personally donated to each recipient in turn, being ladled out from an enormous bin.

There are two interesting postscripts. An eighteenth-century Tichborne interferred with the rules of the bequest; Lady Mabella's threat of seven daughters came true, threatening extinction to the line, and Sir Henry rapidly reverted to tradition! Much more recently when, during and after World War II, bread and flour were rationed and available only against coupons, thousands of unsolicited coupons flowed in, in order that the Tichborne Dole tradition might continue unbroken.

THE BIDDENDEN DOLE, BIDDENDEN
(On A262, 10 miles west of Ashford)

On the village green, at the end of the shop-lined street with its pavements of 'Bethersden marble', there stands a beautifully wrought sign of two women, apparently joined at hip and shoulder. These are the Biddenden Maids, Mary and Eliza Chulkhurst, or Chaulkhurst, the first Siamese twins known to have been born in this country. Their birth date is traditionally said to be 1100 but it is almost certainly nearer to 1400. Mary died at the age of thirty-four; her sister Eliza, inconsolable at her loss, died six hours later. In their joint will they bequeathed their 20 acre field to the church in which they had been baptised and where they had worshipped throughout their lives. The rent from the field was to provide, in perpetuity, an annual dole of bread and cheese for the deserving poor of the parish. It thus came to be known as Bread-and-Cheese Land, a name by which it goes to this day.

In due course part of the field was sold and a number of cottages built on it, known today as the Chulkhurst Estate. The additional revenue has made it possible, in these days of higher prices, to extend the dole to reach a greater number of recipients. For some hundreds of years the dole consisted of two 4lb loaves of bread, 1lb of cheese and also a small purse of money, to each of the parishioners entitled to receive it. Nowadays, in addition to the bread and the cheese, each receives a Biddenden Cake. This is a hard biscuit embossed with an effigy of the Biddenden Maids and bearing their dubious date, 1100. The design of the effigy is old: it was pictorially recorded at least a century and a half ago. The form that the Easter church service takes has been unchanged for just about as long. The dole itself is administered on Easter Monday from the window of one of the 'workhouse' cottages standing on the Bread-and-Cheese Land once owned by the philanthropic Siamese twins. Until comparatively recent times it was a modest ritual, attended only by the vicar and parishioners and friends from the immediately surrounding district. But since the ceremony has come to be generally well known, it has become an object of pilgrimage. So, the sponsors today cater for a far wider range of recipient: anyone who wishes to do so may receive a Biddenden Cake as a memento of the annual occasion.

Lancashire

PACE-EGG ROLLING, PRESTON

The word 'pace' has nothing to do with the speed at which the eggs are rolled; it is older by far than this: a medieval or later corruption of the word Paschal, from the Hebrew *Pasekh,* for Passover. The Paschal Egg, 'perfectly shaped and guarding its secret', has become the traditional Easter Egg, 'eaten', as the church has set on record, 'in thankfulness to Thee, O Lord, on account of Thy Resurrection'.

In a number of places in England, though mainly in the north of the country, as at Barton and Scarborough, the ceremony of egg rolling is still to be seen at Eastertide. It is seen at its most picturesque in Avenham Park, which lies between the centre of Preston and the river Ribble which serpentines past the town to the south. Here, on Easter Monday, crowds assemble to watch children rolling brightly coloured and often most artistically painted hard-boiled eggs down the gentle slope from the trees at the top to the level sward enclosed by shrubs at its foot. The most favoured colours are red and green, but it is naturally the red ones that catch the eye as they roll and bump down the smooth turf. A sense of urgency is engendered by the competition between the eggs of the rival groups of children.

It is generally held that this tradition of egg rolling, or Pace-Egging, as the ceremony is alternatively called, symbolises the rolling aside of the stone blocking the sepulchre from which Christ's resurrection took place. But it may well be that the essential association between eggs and movement lies in the fact that in remote times the egg was, and indeed has remained among simple peoples for many centuries, something mysterious, awe-full: a symbol both of life-contained and of re-birth— as in the renewal of the sense of life with the passing of the dark winter, the growing warmth of the sun and the first appearance of the blades of the primitive crops. Support for this interpretation is lent by the maintenance of the Pace-Egg Mummers' Play in Midgley and other townships of the West Riding of Yorkshire. In these plays St George battles with the Black Prince of Paradine, eventually defeating him; light has triumphed over darkness. Whatever religious overtones may have been laid upon it, the action must date back to pagan times, to the universal worship of a sun god.

BOTTLE KICKING, HALLATON
(Off A47, 10 miles east of Leicester)

The origin of this Easter Monday ceremony possibly dates back to a Saxon Easter Hare ritual, but is generally believed to have sprung from a bargain struck between the vicar and his parishioners. In return for a coveted piece of land he would pay them annually 'a sufficiency of ale, two hare pies and a score and more penny loaves', to be 'scrambled for' on what is locally known as Hare Pie Bank, near the village.

Whatever its origin, today it is an elaborate and noisy affair. After a service, a procession goes to the vicarage, where two hare pies are carved. Some portions go into a sack, the remainder is scrambled for, and anyone obtaining a piece intact can rely on a spell of good fortune. But the day's main activities have yet to commence. They are timed for 2.15 pm, when the Custodian of the Bottle (the bottle being in fact a miniature beer-cask) 'drops' the first of two bottles, both of which have been filled, as a signal for the true scrambling to start. The teams of Hallaton and Medbourne, some 2 miles apart, have then to manhandle the bottle, by any means they care to use, across the stream into one another's territory, the 'goal'. No rules exist; there is no limit to the number of players; the keynote is toughness and stamina. There is no time limit. When a goal is scored, the winners broach the cask and a second one is thrown into the melee. This may well last for many hours, with fresh reinforcements from either side arriving on the scene all the time.

When the second goal has been scored, on whichever side, the contents of the cask are shared as far as possible among the members, strangely enough, of both teams. They gather round the cross on the village green. By tradition, the elected captain of the winning team takes the first pull at the cask, and thus makes sure of a really good drink before what remains is shared out among the contestants. The violence and temporary hostility is now a thing of the past, though it had been inevitable and much in evidence during the long hours of scrambling. Two centuries ago the then vicar of Hallaton tried to put an end to the ritual. But he woke in the morning to find his vicarage daubed with the threatening slogan: NO PIES, NO PARSON. Wisely, he made no further attempt to stop this long-established and highly popular annual occasion.

Lincolnshire

THROWING THE HOOD, HAXEY
(On A161, 14 miles east of Doncaster)

This is certainly one of the most elaborate, as well as the most strenuous, of all the customs traditionally maintained to this day. It is played out on the outskirts of a small village where it is alternatively known as the Haxey Hood Game. It commemorates the tradition that, riding to church on Sunday, Lady de Mowbray lost her red hood. It was retrieved for her by thirteen humble peasants. Gratefully, she bequeathed a 'hide' of land, still known as the Hood-land, to provide the cost of a new red hood to be competed for annually by thirteen villagers. That was 700 years ago.

On 6 January (Plough Monday) every year, at 2 o'clock in the afternoon, the church bells summon King Boggin, his eleven Boggin attendants and the Fool, to the base of the old cross. The Boggins all wear tall hats decked with red flowers, and pink jackets; the King holds a staff-of-office consisting of thirteen willow wands bound with thirteen withies; the Fool, with blackened face, wears a grotesque garb and has coloured streamers flowing from his shoulders. He mounts his rostrum, re-tells the traditional story, and then cries: 'Hoose agen Hoose, Toone agen Toone! If thou meetst a man, hook him doone but dunnut hurt him!' As he speaks, his streamers are set alight: a piece of ritual known as Smoking the Fool, but with obvious overtones of pre-Christian sacrifice. After this, a succession of pieces of tightly-rolled sackcloth, representing hoods, are thrown by King Boggin to the villagers, who fight for them in order to carry them to one or other of the goals, the village inns. If intercepted by a Boggin, the hood is pronounced dead and another is thrown in; if it reaches the selected inn, the bearer receives a shilling and another hood is at once thrown in.

Finally, the 'Sway' commences. Now the whole concourse of men and youths take charge of a massive leather roll, the final hood. Their objective is to convey it to one or other of the two inns. The route is down hill, the struggle increasingly violent, though always good-humoured. It seems that every able-bodied man and boy is engaged in it; they may be so evenly matched, 'Hoose agen Hoose', that the issue long remains in doubt. But the hood reaches its destination at last; there are free drinks for the winners; and the hood remains there until Plough Monday next year.

56

THE CEREMONY OF THE KEYS

It has been said—and so far no military historian has successfully challenged the claim—that this is the oldest military ceremony in the world. It is also surely, the briefest. It has certainly been carried out nightly for no less than 700 years; and as the Tower of London where it takes place, is nearly 200 years older than that, its Main Guard having been formed in 1078, the ceremony may well be substantially older than the seven centuries claimed for it. Ancient though it is, the actual ceremony is extremely brief: it lasts only seven minutes, but it is very well worth watching. Permission to attend may be obtained without undue difficulty by prior application to the Resident Governor of the Tower.

At seven minutes to ten every night of the year a sergeant of the Guards and four other ranks, in dress uniform and bearskin and with bayonets set in their rifles, known as the Escort of the Keys, one of them carrying a lantern, present themselves outside the Bloody Tower, where they are met by the Chief Warder. The whole party then proceeds in turn to the West Gate, the Middle Tower, and the Byward Tower. At each the party halts and, while the Escort presents arms, the Chief Warder locks the gate. They then return to the Bloody Tower, where the sentry on duty challenges: 'Halt! Who comes there?' To the Chief Warder's reply, 'The Keys', the sentry cries: 'Whose keys?' The Chief Warder replies: Queen Elizabeth's Keys.' The sentry then calls out in a loud voice: 'Pass, Queen Elizabeth's Keys. All's well!'

The Chief Warder and the Guards' Escort of the Keys then pass through the archway to the Main Guard. The guard present arms as a military salute to the Keys, and the Chief Warder doffs his hat and cries in ringing tones: 'God preserve Queen Elizabeth!' To this the guard, and the Escort of the Keys, jointly cry: 'Amen!' The timing has been meticulous. It is now exactly 10 o'clock, the hour at which the Tower bugler traditionally sounds the Last Post. The Ceremony of the Keys has been completed. The Chief Warder now carries them to the Queen's House where he hands them over to the Resident Governor of the Tower. Silence falls over the stonegirt precincts until dawn next day.

THE EASTER PARADE

The origin of this very picturesque traditional occasion, known affectionately as the Easter Parade and starting at 3 o'clock in the afternoon of Easter Sunday, is not as remote, or mysterious, as many of the traditions and customs of England; there is no religious, or superstitious significance attached to it whatsoever.

In the year 1829 the somewhat disreputable country district on the outskirts of London known as Battersea Fields was the venue for a duel between the Marquess of Winchester and the Duke of Wellington himself. Word got about, and the elite of London society flocked to the Fields to witness this aristocratic encounter. Neither duellist was injured but 'honour was satisfied', and high society, attired in the height of fashion, had had an unexpected opportunity to show off its finery. Twenty years later the district was cleaned up and made respectable, and re-named Battersea Park. In 1858 Queen Victoria gave it the ultimate cachet of respectability and class by paying it a state visit in the spring. For the occasion she wore, of course, a new spring bonnet and gown. This set the fashion for a display each spring of the newest fashions in millinery and gowns, and from then onwards that tradition has expanded; every society lady vied with her rivals to appear in something more spectacular than anything that had been seen before.

Inevitably the tradition penetrated those who were not high society; today, all who wish can appear in their finery. The original blossoming of mere Easter bonnets has now been elaborated. A succession of ornamental floats, each more decorative than the last, illustrates an annual theme. In 1970 it was holidays. There were people on 'penny-farthings' and 'sociables'; in vintage cars; in rickshaws drawn by kimono-clad Japanese girls. There was the traditional floral float from the Channel Isles, carrying the Easter Princess and her maids of honour. There were wild animals from Windsor Safari Park, clowns from the Chessington Zoo Circus, and a baby elephant. And of course, as always, there was music to stir the heart. Those who attended the 1970 Easter Parade were able to hear one of the finest bands in the country, that of the United States Air Force.

HARNESS HORSE PARADE

The first of the annual Cart or Van Horse Parades was held nearly a century ago in Battersea Park, setting for London's annual Easter Parade. It was restricted to turn-outs that had already won prizes in smaller, local competitions, all of which must have been held within a radius of 7 miles of Charing Cross. In those days, of course, all traffic was horse drawn, and the emphasis was, not unexpectedly, on the great draught horses—the Suffolk Punches for example, and the giant Clydesdales. Comparatively recently, however, the name of the event has been altered to the Harness Horse Parade. This has enabled smaller breeds of horses, such as those that draw the 'totters' carts used for collecting scrap-iron and other expendable commodities from door to door, and also ponies harnessed to private gigs and traps, to enter.

The prime objective of the organisers of the event was 'to promote and maintain high standards of turn-out, both as to horse, vehicle and driver'. The winners received prizes, premiums, diplomas and rosettes awarded by various interested bodies, notably the Royal Society for the Prevention of Cruelty to Animals. Though horsedrawn traffic is not a thousandth part of what it was when the tradition was established in 1886, there are still many horses in regular use (quite apart from those of the army, police and the state coaches used by the Royal Family and the Lord Mayor). Some of the major brewers still use a few big draught horses for their drays; one or two old-established commercial firms, for prestige purposes, employ liveried drivers, smart horses and decorative if old-fashioned light vans; and a few die-hards still maintain one or two four-wheeled carriages or two-wheeled gigs, for special use.

This annual Harness Horse Parade is held in the Inner Circle of Regent's Park, on the morning of Easter Monday. The turn-outs, large and small, assemble at 10.30am for inspection. During the next hour and a half keen eyes are bent on them, some by knowledgeable amateurs, others by the expert official judges. At noon the prizes are awarded. They are distributed among the various categories, in each of which there will have been a number of rival horses and vehicles and their drivers, all so admirably turned out that it takes an expert eye indeed to come to a decision as to which of them is paramount over the rest.

London

THE LORD MAYOR'S SHOW

This magnificent sustained display of civic pride, pomp and circumstance, without question the most spectacular event that ever takes place in London's streets and rivalling even the splendour of the State Opening of Parliament and the State Rides of visiting royalty, takes place on the occasion of the installation in office of each new Lord Mayor of London, on the Saturday of, or immediately following, 9 November. It is a tradition that dates back over seven centuries to the reign of King John, who decreed that London's new Lord Mayor, on election, must publicly present himself to the people as well as to his Sovereign Lord or, in his absence, to the Royal Justices. Once he rode a horse; he even travelled along London's river. But for two centuries past he has always been conveyed, with escort, by state coach.

With each succeeding year the procession becomes more eye-catching in splendour and originality. The newly elected Lord Mayor journeys from the Mansion House to the Royal Courts of Justice where, at exactly midday, he swears before the Lord Chief Justice and Bench that he will dutifully carry out those responsibilities entailed by his high-ranking office. He then invites the justices to dine with him later on at Guildhall. Then he begins the circuitous return to the Mansion House, which has been the official Lord Mayoral residence for more than 200 years.

The glory of the procession, which takes a full half hour to pass any given point, is impossible to convey in mere words. The Lord Mayor rides in a 'Cinderella'-type state coach, lavishly gilded, driven by a be-wigged coachman and drawn by six Shire horses. He is accompanied by the City Marshal, in the saddle, and by his servants in full and glittering livery. He has a bodyguard, the Company of Pikemen and Musketeers, drawn from the Honourable Artillery Company but wearing historic uniforms, armour, helmets and pikes. They walk beside and behind the mayoral coach, bringing up the rear of the mile-long procession that consists of a number of ornamental floats on which the new Lord Mayor's selected theme—shipping, exporting, or whatever—is depicted three-dimensionally by ingeniously conceived tableaux built up like small theatre sets, with male and female characters to grace them.

64

OAK APPLE DAY, ROYAL HOSPITAL, CHELSEA

Oak Apple Day, 29 May, is the anniversary of the birthday of King Charles II who founded the Royal Hospital, Chelsea, home of the Chelsea Pensioners, built almost 300 years ago by the great architect of London, Sir Christopher Wren. The anniversary is remembered annually as Founder's Day at the hospital, when the In-Pensioners honour their royal founder. It is additionally fitting that this should be the day of the ceremony since 29 May is the day on which Charles II's escape after the Battle of Worcester, and his day-long concealment in the Boscobel Oak, are also commemorated. Oak and oak-apples have always been associated with this monarch.

In the nobly proportioned Figure Court of the Royal Hospital there stands the equestrian statue of Charles II. For this remembrance day it is liberally decked with oak leaves and set about with oak branches. In the Court some 400 Pensioners parade for the occasion. Though their average age may well be in excess of seventy, and many of them are in their nineties, they are smart and alert in their scarlet uniforms, each bedecked with a sprig of oak. On parade they are formally inspected, either by a member of the Royal Family (in this case Princess Alexandra) or by some high-ranking officer. An address is given, and this is followed by three cheers, first for 'Our Pious Founder, King Charles', and then for 'Her Majesty'.

The Royal Hospital itself is then officially inspected, while military bands play martial music in the Figure Court. After the official inspection, the hospital is open for inspection by the casual visitor, who will be able to see for himself how excellently maintained this three-centuries-old building, established for worthy veterans of the armed services, proves to be. Meanwhile, what may well be regarded by many of the men as an equally important part of the ritual is about to begin: the traditional plum pudding and pint of beer which each In-Pensioner is entitled to. They have heard the address; rheumatic or not, they have paraded smartly; they have raised three cheers for their Pious Founder and for the reigning monarch. Now, at last, well-loved pipes can be lit and they can settle down again to talk, as they love to do, of army life in an older tradition and of 'battles long ago'.

THE ROYAL MAUNDY

The annual distribution of the Royal Maundy money by the reigning sovereign is an ancient, and the most important, of the many doles of money or goods to deserving poor under various bequests. The word 'maundy' derives from the Latin *mandatum* and refers to Christ's 'A new commandment I give you, that ye love one another,' spoken as He washed His disciples' feet at the Last Supper, in token of humility. For many centuries the ceremony included actually washing the feet of the chosen poor by the monarch; Edward II is known to have done it six centuries ago; James II was probably the last monarch actually to do so. Four centuries ago Edward III instituted the practice of distributing *maunds,* or doles, to as many men and women as the years he had lived. They consisted of food and clothing, but were later replaced by money.

Today, alternately in Westminster Abbey and certain other churches such as St George's Chapel, Windsor, and Southwark Cathedral, a modified but still elaborate version of the ceremony is annually carried out on Maundy Thursday, the day before Good Friday. With the Yeomen of the Guard in attendance, Her Majesty the Queen leads a procession of clergy down the choir between the two rows of recipients, whose numbers tally with the years of her age. They carry posies: a reminder that in olden times this was done as a safeguard against the risk of fever and infection. A Yeoman carried a gold dish containing the appropriate number of small leather draw-string purses, some red, some white, two for each recipient. The white ones contain specially minted Maundy Money: small silver coins to the value of one penny, twopence, threepence and fourpence; the number of coins also tallies with the Queen's age. The red purses contain money representing the now-discontinued gifts of food and clothing: the men receive nearly £5, the women rather less. To some this may seem unreasonable

The recipients are handed their purses by the Queen. The coins are legal tender but it is rare for them to be spent—though numismatists are always eager to pay high prices for complete sets. Feasting and revelry used once to attend this ceremony, but was discontinued before Victoria came to the throne. The emphasis, today, is on royal humility in circumstances of grandeur and pomp.

London

TROOPING THE COLOUR

This traditional ceremony is the most spectacular, the most heart-stirring, of all the displays of military pageantry to be seen in this country—and perhaps in any other country in the world. It is held on what is known as the Queen's 'official birthday', nowadays the second Saturday in June. The venue is the Horse Guards Parade, off White-hall, within a stone's throw of the Cenotaph; the occasion is mounted by the Brigade of Guards. Today, and indeed for the past 200 years since it was instituted by George II, it has been regarded as a loyal salute to the reigning sovereign; but its origins go a good deal further back than the mid-eighteenth century. Before that, the 'colours'—to which a man was called to serve his king and country—were used on the field of battle as a rallying-point; in time of peace the colours were laid up, or lodged, at the regiment's or battalion's headquarters. So there developed the ceremony known as 'Lodging the Colours', and this came to be associated with the guard-mounting carried out tradition-ally by the Brigade of Guards.

Her Majesty the Queen is Colonel-in-Chief of a number of regi-ments, including the Life Guards, the Royal Horse Guards (also known as The Blues), the Grenadier and Coldstream Guards, the Scots, Welsh and Irish Guards. Prior to the Trooping of the Colour she rides from Buckingham Palace to Horse Guards Parade, attended by a Sover-eign's Mounted Escort. Meanwhile the Brigade of Guards and the Household Cavalry are massed on the parade ground, awaiting her arrival. She wears the uniform of one of the regiments of which she is Colonel-in-Chief, and has her own mounted escort of one officer as she inspects the Guards. Then, to the martial music of the massed bands, and still attended, she takes the salute.

Only one Colour is trooped annually, that of each regiment in very strict rotation. It is interesting to note that the term Lodging was changed to Trooping because the music that accompanied the act was known as a Troop. The ceremony over, the Queen returns to Bucking-ham Palace at the head of her guards, who, again in strict rotation, are commissioned to undertake to mount the palace guard, a duty which there is always keen rivalry among them to fulfil.

MAY MORNING ON MAGDALEN TOWER, OXFORD

Sun worship is a tradition that goes so far back into the mists of time, and is so universal, that no scholar, however eminent, has ever established when it started. It was a religion in ancient Egypt, where the ceremonies were performed as close to the sun as possible. The eighteenth-dynasty Egyptian King Akhenaten would stand on a tower to receive, on his lips and eyelids, the first rays of the sun as it appeared over the eastern horizon. So, the ceremony that has taken place in Oxford for some centuries, perhaps first held to mark the completion of the beautiful 144ft high tower in 1501, though old by Western standards is still relatively new. It is a greeting of the sun on the first morning of the month, rather than a pagan act of sun worship.

At exactly 6 o'clock in the morning of 1 May every year the white-surpliced choristers of Magdalen College Chapel, assembled between the pinnacles of the tower, break into a *Te Deum*, which they traditionally sing in Latin: *Te Deum Patrem Collimus.* It was composed especially for this ceremony more than 300 years ago, by a Fellow of the college, which was founded as long ago as 1458. Prior to this special *Te Deum*, up to the time of the Reformation this annual ceremony had taken the form of a requiem mass for the soul of Henry VII.

The service is immediately followed by a peal from the famous Magdalen College bells. On a still morning, such as is usual on 1 May, they can be heard far and wide across the city roofs and the Isis, as the Thames is known in the region of Oxford. They are the signal for what has been a religious ceremony (replacing what was an essentially pagan one) to be translated into secular terms. Town and Gown alike take part in this festival. In the streets there are displays of traditional dancing by the long-established morris dancers; the Cherwell, that small, picturesque tributary of the Isis that flows idly beneath the arches of Magdalen Bridges carrying the famous 'High' past the foot of the tower, is crowded with punts and canoes and other small river craft, all filled to capacity with those who have risen early to play their own spectator part within sight and sound of the service on Magdalen Chapel Tower whose origins lie secreted in the 'dark backward and abysm of time'.

MORRIS DANCING AT BAMPTON
(10 miles west of Oxford)

Morris dancing remains a feature of the English countryside that has survived many centuries. It is to be found as far north as Yorkshire, in the Midlands, in Somerset and farther into the Westcountry. It is claimed in Bampton that it has thrived there for 500 years at least. Like so many ceremonies in which strenuous motion is involved, the true origin is almost certainly pagan: dancing was associated with the urge to fertility in human beings, animals and crops.

On Whit Monday at Bampton the team of men (women are never included in either morris dancing or sword dancing) sets out at breakfast time from the village square to dance virtually throughout the day, up and down the streets, through gardens, to end, customarily, on the vicarage lawn where they enjoy a well-earned tea. They dance to the lively music of fiddle and accordion (replacing the older tabor and pipe); they wear white trousers and white shirts, with gay braiding or more elaborate garlands criss-crossing their breasts. On the lower trouser-legs are sewn leather patches on which are mounted small bells that jingle tunefully as they dance. They wear white hats, in various local traditional styles, often decorated with flowers. This all-white garb is the more effective when, as is often the case, certain of the dancers' faces are blacked; it is this tradition that leads some to suppose that 'morris' is a corruption of 'moorish', especially as the style of the dance is primitive. In fact the form the dance takes, like the tradition, is truly English.

The men no longer always carry either swords or staves, as morris dancers did generations ago; but they make elaborate play overhead with handkerchiefs. Some, notably at Wells in Somerset, retain the staves, however. The dancing is often accompanied by the buffooneries of the Fool, sometimes with bladder on stick; Robin Hood and Maid Marian (always a male) are traditionally present; so too, often, is the hobby-horse. At Bampton a sword-bearer distributes slices of cake among the womenfolk—a further reminder that the origin of the occasion was associated with fertility and the hunt. Not surprisingly, there are regional differences in both attire and style of dancing; but the essence of this picturesque traditional custom remains the same.

APPLE WASSAILING, CARHAMPTON
(On A39, 4 miles south-east of Minehead)

The old-fashioned word 'wassail' is a partially modernised form of the Anglo-Saxon *Waes-hal!* and means, quite simply: 'Be in good health!' It is a wish that is, today, generally expressed when one party greets another and drinks to its wellbeing; it is more closely identified with winter-time traditions than with any others. One of its more picturesque rituals is that of wishing good health to cider-apple trees.

The ceremony takes place in Carhampton after night has fallen on 17 January (Twelfth Night, by the old calendar), when the inhabitants of this hamlet in the heart of the cider-producing country assemble and move in procession to one of the many apple orchards in the district. A representative tree, always a well-grown one, has already been selected. The men form a close circle about it. One of them carries a pail full of last year's cider. Into this a number of pieces of toast are dipped, and then hung on the lower branches and in the forks of the tree. These are ritual gifts 'to the robins', who represent the good spirits of the trees; that they are soaked in cider is a hint to the good spirits 'for the future'. But there must also be a warning to the potential evil spirits. This, in olden times, almost certainly consisted of a shower of stones thrown up into the branches; today it consists of a few volleys of shot-gun fire, which will do no harm at all as the tree at the time is bare.

Then, as a further hint, cider is thrown in cup-fulls from the pail over the lower branches, to serve this time as a healing balm. Meanwhile the wassailers break into a traditional chant, a set of doggerel verses of which the refrain is 'Old Apple Tree, Old Apple Tree, We're come to wassail Thee!' The chant is sometimes accompanied by accordion or other instrument. After the chant, the remainder of the cider in the pail is shared out among the wassailers, who drink one another's health, coupled with that of the orchard trees as a whole. It is easy to see where the roots of this ritual lie. Today, Somerset's economy may not depend exclusively on the flourishing of its apple orchards; but the basic notion of a crop that may be good (and so life-saving) or bad (and so death-bringing) is implicit in the gestures that combine supplication and threat: the sprinkling of cider, and volleys of small-shot.

PUNKY NIGHT, HINTON ST GEORGE
(Off A30, 2 miles north of Crewkerne)

Hallowe'en is 31 October, the eve of 1 November, All Saints' Day. But the inhabitants of this small village, and certainly the children, are unlikely to know the origin of the light-hearted occasion which takes place there. Few if any of them will know that All Hallows in the ancient Celtic calendar marked the onset of true winter and New Year. Hallowe'en was New Year's Eve; the apparently dying sun was 'encouraged' to revive by the lighting of bonfires, by chanting and incantations and strenuous dancing.

Today, the bonfires of a pagan festival have been shifted on to Guy Fawkes Night, nearly a week later, but something of the old tradition survives, though it takes modified and various forms. In the North of England it may be called Nut-Crack Night, or Dookie-Apple Night; elsewhere it is called Apple and Candle Night. The nuts are chestnuts, roasted in the embers, their bursting interpreted into promises and omens. The apples must be bobbed for, and snatched at with the teeth, either in a tub of water or revolving over a candle flame: light and promise once again.

In this village, in whose name England's Patron Saint is proudly remembered, Hallowe'en, in spite of its part-pagan, part-religious origin, is largely a festival for the children. It is they who carry the 'punkies', the curiously contrived candle-lanterns made from large mangel-wurzels hollowed out and windowed so that the candles inserted in them can be brightly seen. It is a matter of pride among them that they design and make their own punkies, though some parental help may be given.

Armed with their lanterns, the children parade through the village after nightfall, knocking on the door of each cottage in turn, singing as they go, and hoping for either a coin or a new candle to be given at each doorstep in return for their song. An echo of the religious aspect of the custom, the church's eventual acceptance of a pre-Christian ceremony which it tried for a long while to stamp out, lies in the fact that this door-to-door parade of singing children was known until comparatively recently, and is still referred to by some of the older villagers, as 'souling': singing for the souls of those who have passed away.

HORN DANCERS AT ABBOTS BROMLEY
(10 miles north of Lichfield)

The first Monday after 4 September is the date of this annual occasion, so ancient that its origin almost certainly dates from prehistoric times when men donned animal skins to ensure success in the chase. The reindeer antlers worn are certainly British—and reindeer became extinct in England before the Norman Conquest. The festival is recorded in the thirteenth century and was most probably instituted in the reign of Henry III to symbolise the restoring of forest rights to the men of the village that lies in the heart of what was once the Royal Forest of Needwood. Here, 1,000 years ago, reindeer are known to have been plentiful. As early as the seventeenth century the occasion was recorded in detail; the ceremony has changed but little.

Twelve men traditionally take part in the dance. Six of them carry on their heads great reindeer antlers, the largest having a span of more than 3ft weighing more than 25lb. They are accompanied by Robin Hood with his bow, Maid Marian with her collecting-ladle, the Fool with his cap and bells, the Boy with his triangle, the Hobby-horse man with his clapper-jaws, and the Musician with his accordion, replacing the old pipe and tabor. The dancers wear a garb derived from Tudor times: a wide beret, a green shirt beneath a thigh-length jerkin, knee-breeches on which a pattern of oak-leaves is appliqued, and woollen stockings.

At 8.30 in the morning the six pairs of antlers are collected from the chapel, in which they have been hung for the past year, and the dance begins. It will last, with brief intervals for much-needed refreshment, for twelve hours. During that time the men will have danced not only on the green but at farms and hamlets and a stately home near by, covering a parish circuit of not much less than 20 miles. It is a gruelling test of stamina, but competition for inclusion in The Six is always keen. The dance itself is stereotyped: first a ring, then a broken loop, from which the horn bearers, in pairs, advance towards one another, and retreat, the tips of their horns almost touching as they do so. There is of course an echo here of the remote origin of the symbolic dancing: this was challenge to combat, and a man killed his prey—or was himself killed by it while seeking food for his family.

Staffordshire

THE GREENHILL BOWER, LICHFIELD
(On A51, 16 miles north of Birmingham)

The origins of this charmingly named and most attractive floral occasion are lost in the mists of time. Probably they date back to pre-Christian days, but this cannot be proved. Locally, at any rate, it is more generally associated with the founding of the first bishopric here in the Kingdom of Mercia (the Midlands) by the victorious King of Northumbria; and that was almost exactly 1,300 years ago.

The Greenhill Bower, however, has come to be identified with another very ancient tradition in this Midlands town dominated by the three 'Ladies of the Vale'—the triple spires of its ancient and beautiful cathedral which are a landmark for miles in every direction. This was the 'Court of Arraye of Men and Arms', which dates back to 1285, the reign of Edward I, and the Statute of Winchester. This ordained that in return for certain privileges in respect of trading, the town must provide a given 'weight' of armour and weaponry, to be worn and used when called upon by a given number of freemen aged not less than fifteen years old. They must parade, and the arms and weaponry be inspected and approved, once a year by this Court of Arraye. It was a heavy imposition on a small town, and one which lasted for more than 300 years, spanning no fewer than sixteen Plantagenet and Tudor reigns.

The Court of Arraye ceased to exist three and a half centuries ago but it is remembered annually on Whit Monday, when a given number of Lichfield's citizenry parade in the streets wearing suits of armour which can range from relatively lightweight chain-mail to the full panoply of helmet, breastplate, cuisses and greaves. In these days of computerised and progressively 'in-humanised' warfare, such goings-on may seem absurd rather than impressive, and it is possible that many of those taking part in the combined ceremony of Court of Arraye and Greenhill Bower may feel faintly sheepish as they do so. Perhaps that is why, increasingly, the accent today is on display of ornamental floats and fancy-dress, particularly among the younger element. But the older inhabitants, looking up at their cherished Early English cathedral of rose-red stone, may vaguely recall that the prime objective all those centuries ago was 'to preserve these ancient walls against the aggressor'.

HOT-PENNY SCRAMBLING, RYE
(On A259, 11 miles north-east of Hastings)

Like its neighbour Winchelsea, a mile or two to the west, this most picturesque small town was left high and dry many centuries ago when the waters of the English Channel receded down the estuary of the Rother. So it is strange to reflect that, like Winchelsea, Hastings, Romney, Hythe, Sandwich and Dover, Rye was one of the famous Cinque Ports, established even longer ago. In return for certain privileges granted to them by the monarch (privileges retained by them until within the last 150 years) they undertook to supply men and ships when needed for the defence of the vulnerable southern coastline. Today, within the remains of its ancient walls, its medieval Land Gate and Ypres Tower, Rye sleeps unmindful of the days when it was a thriving sea port.

Once every year, however, it comes very much to life. The occasion is Mayoring Day, towards the end of May, on or about 23rd of the month. On this day the mayor in his ceremonial robes of office, his aldermen and town councillors, take their stand either at a window of the town hall or sometimes on a balcony of the George Inn; the clocks strike the hour of noon, and this is the signal for quantities of hot pennies to be thrown from window or balcony down to the swarms of Rye children milling about, expectant and vociferous, in the street immediately below.

Antiquarians have attempted to establish the origin of this traditional distribution of hot coins, but without reaching any firm conclusion. One theory is that it symbolises the honest bribery indulged in at times of election, whether parliamentary or mayoral: a gesture to keep the electorate sweet. More probably, however, it is a tradition maintained to keep fresh in people's minds the knowledge that in its heyday Rye was a town regarded as of sufficient importance to possess its own mint and issue its own coin of the realm. To this day a prolongation of the High Street, just short of where the medieval Strand Gate formerly stood, is called The Mint. The coins thrown—pennies only—having been baked prior to being distributed at random to be scrambled for by anyone not caring whether or not his palms and fingers are scorched as a result, were originally hot from the mint.

MARBLES CHAMPIONSHIP, TINSLEY GREEN
(Off B2036, 6 miles south of Redhill)

This self-styled British Individual Marbles Championship (in which for the first time in 1970 teams from USA and Mexico competed) is played annually on Good Friday in a small hamlet lying sequestered off a minor road yet within earshot of the big jets flying in and out of nearby Gatwick airport. It started round about the year 1600, when, tradition says, two men of the district competed with one another for the hand of a village maiden. They ran, jumped, wrestled and engaged in other strenuous forms of sport, but at the end of each bout they were adjudged equal winners. They therefore resorted to the game of marbles, a simple game usually played by children though known to the Romans 2,000 years earlier. As a result of one long-protracted game, one of the two suitors for the maiden's hand was acclaimed winner, and got his bride.

The venue of the championship is a circular sanded ring, or rink, 6ft in diameter, outside the Greyhound inn. In the middle of the ring, forty-nine marbles are placed. Teams of six competitors, each furnished with a 'tolley'—a $\frac{3}{4}$in glass marble—seek to dislodge from the ring as many of the marbles as possible, but without losing their own. Each competitor continues until his tolley is lost, when he must hand over to the next in order. There are strict rules as to the 'shooting', or 'flicking', of the tolley : only the thumb and index-finger may be used, and there must be no 'fudging'—movement of any other part of the hand. The highest individual scorer in each bout then challenges the others, and the winner then challenges the previous year's champion for a final bout to decide the current year's Individual Champion of Britain. In this final bout only thirteen marbles are placed in the ring, for ejection by the competitors' tolleys. This in fact means seven times 'lucky number 7' for the preliminary bouts; 'unlucky 13' for the deciding bout.

The championship is taken with the greatest possible seriousness—even though it is more than possible that any but the oldest players (and they retain a good eye and dexterity in Tinsley Green to a ripe old age !) may have forgotten completely the origin of the championship. There is no possibility of cheating, with so close-set an audience; proceedings are actually checked by the British Marbles Control Board.

NATIONAL TOWN CRIERS' CHAMPIONSHIP, HASTINGS

The office of Town Crier (now, of course, defunct) was for centuries of immense importance. It originated in the Middle Ages as the only practicable means of imparting instructions, warnings and information of all kinds to a largely illiterate populace. Tewkesbury in Gloucestershire had a Town Crier in the sixteenth century; Guildford in Surrey had one in the early fifteenth century; Kirkham in Lancashire, and Alcester in Warwickshire, had Town Criers in the thirteenth century; and Marlborough in Wiltshire, and Hastings in Sussex, had Town Criers as long ago as the years 1204 and 1205. It is fitting, therefore, that the annual championships held nowadays for competitors in this ancient tradition should be held in Hastings, where in fact for the past quarter of a century and more the brazen-throated men meet annually in mid-August.

They come from far and wide : men with stentorian voices beside whom the best professional toast-masters seem mere whisperers. They wear, as did their ancestors in the far-off days when this office was vital to the smooth-running of a community, antiquated costumes. There are knee-breeches and white stockings for some; top hats and cocked hats with cockades; frills and flounced cravats; buckled shoes and half-boots; brocaded tunics and semi-military uniforms; gold buttons the size of doubloons and an array of medals that perhaps should not always be looked at too closely !

They brandish a hand-bell apiece—the traditional gathering-signal for all within earshot to attend and hear. Their warning cry, of course, is a full-throated 'OYEZ! OYEZ!! OYEZ!!!' This is a corruption of the medieval French command to 'give ear'. They parade in strength, to compete in the presence of well qualified judges and personalities from the world of entertainment. There are four main money prizes, and additional prizes and bonuses for 'turn-out'. There is an annual Challenge Cup presented by a famous Sunday newspaper, and the outright winner receives a replica of the cup 'for keeps', as well as his prize in money. Some winners become Honorary Town Criers of American townships. In 1969 the theme of the test piece was a 'Salute to the fearless astronauts who placed a plaque on the moon stating that they Came in Peace for All Mankind'. And the last words declaimed, as for centuries past, are always 'God Save the Queen!' (or King).

SWAN-UPPING

Ever since its introduction into England some time about the twelfth century, the swan has been regarded as a royal bird. Elizabeth I decreed that no one but the monarch might own a swan, but she made two exceptions : the ancient livery companies, the Vintners and the Dyers, were permitted each to own 'a game of swans'—perhaps because before the Great Fire of 1666 their halls had stood on the banks of the Thames.

Annually, on or near the last Monday in July, the ceremony of swan 'upping', or 'hopping', is carried out, to maintain the royal prerogative and establish the rightful ownership of every cygnet hatched on the river between London Bridge and Henley, 36 miles upstream, in the past year. In an average year there may be as many as 500 and more cygnets to be identified and appropriately marked.

The colourful ceremony necessarily lasts several days. There is a procession of six skiffs, the first two of which fly the Queen's standard. The Queen's Swan Keeper, or Master, in scarlet livery and wearing a feather behind the badge on his peaked cap, commands the convoy. Two skiffs follow, representing the Vintners, with their Swan Master in green livery, and two more representing the Dyers, with their Swan Master in a livery of blue. The skiffs are rowed by oarsmen in variegated jerseys and caps, sometimes in stripes and in a variety of red, white and blue tones. Red, white and blue, again, are the colours borne by the skiffs, and all carry the emblem of the Royal Swan; the white flags also carry a golden crown and the royal emblem EIIR.

Every cygnet must be traced. The monarch's are left, like their parents, un-'nicked'; the Dyers' cygnets are nicked on one side of the bill; the Vintners' cygnets on each side of the bill, as were their parents. If there is difficulty in establishing ownership, then the livery companies take each in turn; if there is mixed parenthood, again the cygnets are claimed by each company turn and turn about; the odd cygnet is always attributed to the cob (male swan) not to the pen. With nearly 40 miles of broad river to 'sweep', this ceremony inevitably takes time. Formerly it was attended by much boisterous revelry; today it is no less picturesque than it used to be, but it is carried out more decorously on both river bank and water alike.

MOP FAIR, STRATFORD-ON-AVON

Mop Fair dates back to the fourteenth century when, as a result of the Black Death, a desperate shortage of able-bodied labourers caused Edward III to decree that all fit men should offer themselves at the nearest fair or market, primarily for work in agriculture. In the course of time this became simply a general hiring fair, and this in turn became largely an occasion when maid-servants offered themselves for employment in the great houses. To begin with, the fair had been known as the Statute Fair (colloquially 'Statty' Fair); but, probably because the maid-servants carried the traditional bunch of rags or coarse wool symbolising the type of service they were offering, the name changed. 'Mrs Mopp' today, is an affectionate echo of this.

And today, the centuries-old tradition of hiring onself out for fifty-two (or sometimes, as a safeguard against exploitation, for fifty-one) weeks has long been replaced by the advertisement column and the Labour Exchange. But not so the occasion—at least in Midland counties. The original Mop Fairs incorporated, as did so many high days and holidays down the centuries, various ancillary activities, especially games, sports and boisterous entertainment. In Stratford-on-Avon the traditional elements, admittedly in modified form, may still be witnessed on 12 October, and country-style dancing is an important feature in streets and open spaces.

For the thousands of visitors to Shakespeare's birthplace, on this date anyway—some six months after the annual celebrations of the Bard of Avon's birthday on 23 April, which to Shakespeare lovers the world over is much more significant than any Mop Fair—the high-spot of the day's festivities is the roasting of the ox. Gone are the spacious days when no fewer than eight oxen would be publicly roasted and partaken of by all and sundry, with eight fat pigs, too, to fill up the corners in stomachs more accustomed to self-indulgence at table than ours. You may, however, share from side-stalls in the lavish eating that goes on. You will be in good company, too : the town's mayor, in full regalia and attended by his mace-bearer and other dignitaries, will be present, and officiate with sharpened carving-knife, at this rare but flourishing English Mop Fair.

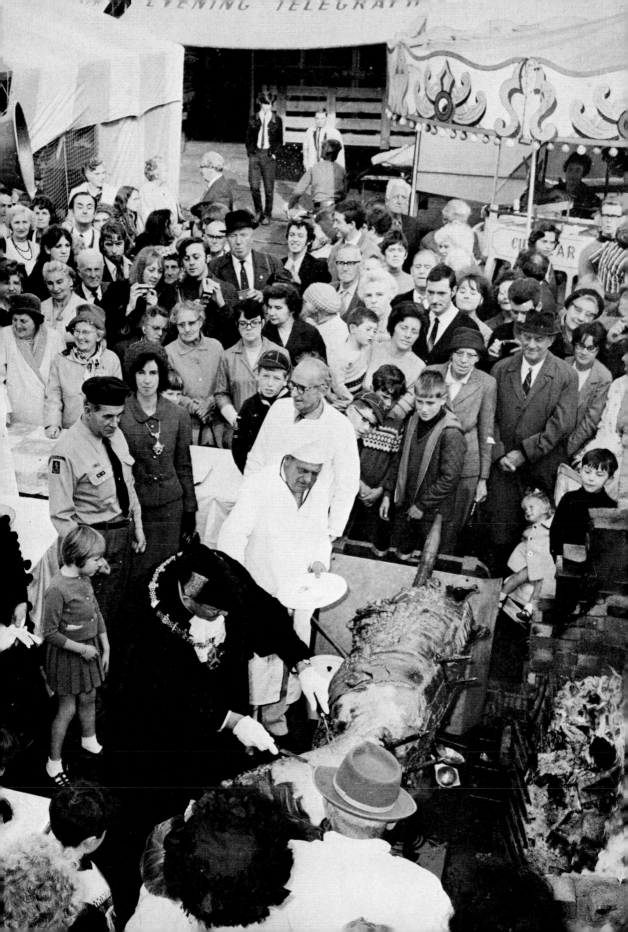

Westmorland

THE GUIDES' RACE, GRASMERE

You might think that sports hardly come into the category of custom and tradition. In fact, the sports held near the picturesque village of Grasmere can justify a claim to be traditional in that not only were they instituted more than a century ago but two of their high spots are the 1,000-year-old Cumberland-and-Westmorland-style wrestling, and the famous Guides' Race first run almost exactly a century ago.

These Lakeland sports are held annually on the Thursday nearest to 20 August, in a beautiful natural arena on the outskirts of the village. In six hours, starting at noon when they are officially announced by a be-smocked bell-man, some twenty events take place, including short- and long-distance races, long, high and pole-vaulting, all to the music of the traditional drum and fife band. But for the vast majority of those attending the sports, the wrestling, in various categories from heavy-weight down to fourteen-year-old boys, is the most important item. Its style is peculiar to the region. Competitors wear off-white singlets and underpants and dark 'drawers'. Their take-up stance is a one-over-one-under grip, each wrestler's hands meeting and locking behind his opponent's back, while each rests his chin on the others shoulder. The stance once approved by the referee, each seeks to throw the other from that locked position and to avoid being twisted so as to fall underneath. There are substantial prizes in all weights, a challenge cup to be competed for, and a special prize for the best competitor of the day, irrespective of category.

The most spectacular event, however, is the Guides Race, which is breathtaking in the extreme. Young men, rigorously trained, race up the steep slope of the 1,500ft Butter Crag, along the indented ridge and sheer down the treacherous scree back to the oval again, a total distance of 2 miles. It is a gruelling test of sheer strength, stamina, fitness and sure-footedness, for the upward slope is overgrown with bracken, the high ridge may be shrouded in mist hiding loose boulders, and the scree is notoriously dangerous even for the most practised and expert competitor. It is a miracle that more ankles are not broken during this race; and it is small wonder that the winner is traditionally hailed by the band playing at full blast : 'See the Conquering Hero Comes!'

Westmorland

RUSH BEARING, AMBLESIDE
(On A591, 4 miles north of Windermere)

This picturesque ceremony may be witnessed in a number of north-western villages, such as Warcop and Musgrave on the east side of the county, and in small townships such as Grasmere and, particularly, Ambleside, in the heart of the Lake District. It derives from medieval times when rushes were the natural floor covering for houses large and small and were used also in churches to spare the worshippers' feet from the cold stone slabs. Rushes were garnered for general use; but priority was always given to the needs of the church, the focal point of communal life. To it, white-robed maidens brought offerings of rushes decked with flowers and ribbons, to be accepted by the priest. Once the religious service that followed was over, the remainder of the day, as on so many communal occasions, was given up to festivities.

The ceremony today, always held on the Saturday nearest to 26 July, the Feast of St Anne, is more elaborate than it used to be, though it still nicely blends the secular and the sacred. The rushes now have no utilitarian purpose, so they are no longer carried in bundles suitable for laying on the stone floor. Instead, they are made up on wooden frames of considerable elaborateness and in such a fashion that they represent symbolic patterns and ornamental designs. These are the Rush Bearings, further adorned with flowers and other decorative devices often so intricate that they almost conceal the rushes. The children are the bearers in the procession that winds through the streets to the church. They pause in the market place, and there a hymn is sung which was composed well over 100 years ago by an Ambleside priest who was a friend of the Lakeland poet, Wordsworth. In it they speak of 'The House of God, As yet a building rude', to which their forefathers 'Bore offerings from the flowery sod, And fragrant rushes strew'd'. They speak of the 'pious lesson given', and promise to 'honour still, together met, The Lord of Earth and Heaven'.

From the market place the procession continues on its way to St Mary's Parish Church, where the Bearings are presented, received by the priest, and deposited in the church. A brief service follows, then the day is wide open for jollifications of various kinds, including the presentation of squares of gingerbread to the bearers.

Wiltshire

DRUIDS RITES AT STONEHENGE
(On A344, 3 miles west of Amesbury)

This colossal megalithic complex, standing proud and silent on Salisbury Plain, was erected some 4,000 years ago by Bronze Age man : a pagan temple for sun worshipping of heroic proportions, 'almost twice as old as Christianity'. Two thousand years ago the Druids, the priests or soothsayers attached to the Celtic tribes in pre-Roman Gaul and Britain, adopted it for their own ritualistic purposes. For centuries past the modern English Druids, the Ancient Order of Druid Hermetists, have celebrated their traditional rites within the circle of enormous trilithons, assembling on Midsummer Eve to keep vigil throughout the night so as to see dawn break over the Hele (or Sun) Stone and then hold a service at the Altar Stone on which, in ancient times, it is generally believed that a victim was sacrificed as the first ray stabbed down. It is true that, in this mid-twentieth century, the Altar and the Hele Stone are no longer in exact alignment at that moment; but astronomers have proved that they would have been 4,000 years ago, when Stonehenge was conceived and built.

It is perhaps even more colourful as a ceremony today that it was then; and less macabre. The Ancient Order of Druids are garbed in flowing white robes, their heads partially covered with white hoods resembling those worn by certain orders of nuns. Robes and hoods are variously adorned and the adornment is matched by the brightly coloured banners that are carried in the procession as it weaves its way among the monoliths and beneath the vast stone lintels placed there by primitive man without the aid of any of the mechanical devices available to his remote descendants today. Sprigs of holly and mistletoe too, those most powerful of traditional growths, are in evidence among members of the gathering as they sing their hymns and speak their ancient incantations.

Probably not one in a hundred of the crowds of spectators who converge from all parts upon Stonehenge either knows or cares to know what it is all about; nevertheless, all unwittingly, spectators and Druids alike are taking part in one of the most ancient and fundamental ceremonies in the world's calendar. It is one that links Britain with Egypt, with Mithras, with all the scattered and long-forgotten prehistoric communities which, in their several fashions over the ages, have worshipped the life-giving Sun God.

THE GROVELY PROCESSION, WISHFORD MAGNA

(5 miles north-west of Salisbury)

On Oak Apple Day, 29 May, the inhabitants of this small village in the Wylye Valley commemorate annually the Royal Charter granted to their forefathers in 1603, entitling them officially to graze their swine, as they had anyway done since Saxon days, beneath the oaks of the then extensive Grovely Forest. It also entitled every man to collect firewood and, once a year, to cut and bear away the largest bough he was capable of carrying back to his cottage. This right was in perpetuity; it has been acknowledged with annual thanksgiving for more than three and a half centuries.

The ceremony starts at noon from a tree on the south side of the village, but the firewood which is its essential feature will have been cut early that morning. A local band heads a procession made up of every able-bodied man, woman and child. The men are bent beneath the weight of outsize boughs of oak, laboriously sawn off. The women, often wearing fancy costumes in antiquated vein, carry on their heads elaborate 'trays' made of interwoven small branches and twigs, symbolising the tight faggots which were so important to their ancestors even only a few short years ago. Many of the children wear quite elaborate fancy dress, often representing considerable ingenuity on the part of those parents who designed and made them.

In olden times a deputation from the village carried a ceremonial faggot to Salisbury. There, after a ritualistic dance, the faggot was ceremoniously laid at the foot of the High Altar of the Cathedral. This dance may well have had its origins far back in time, when superstition was a form of religion. Today that ancient ceremony is discontinued but bundles of firewood are still laid at the cottage doors of the needy, which are often decorated with patterns of oak leaves.

This association with Oak Apple Day is emphasised by the patterns of oak leaves that adorn the large white banners carried at the head of the procession and surround the slogan emblazoned on them: 'Grovely, Grovely, Grovely and All Grovely!' To which, doubtless because, traditionally, the tightly bound faggot is a symbol of strength, there is added the well-tried maxim: 'Unity Is Strenth'. The procession over, the remainder of the day is given up to sport and general festivities.

KIPLINGCOTES DERBY, MIDDLETON-ON-THE-WOLDS
(Off A163, 24 miles east of York)

As the word 'Derby' suggests, this is a horse race—though it has very little in common with the Derby run annually in June on the Epsom racecourse. It is, however, the oldest traditional horse race in Britain, and probably in the world. Moreover, it has one peculiar feature that singles it out from **all** other races the world over: the prize money goes, not to the winner but the runner who comes in **second!**

The race is over an indeterminate course passing through four or five parishes in the East Riding of Yorkshire. It starts at South Dalton at noon on the third Thursday in March and finishes by 1 o'clock at a winning-post at the western end of the parish of Middleton-on-the Wolds, near an old farm from which the race derives its name. (There is a tiny railway-halt nearby, bearing the same name as the farm.)

The prize in this odd race, which has been run ever since 1519, is competed for by not more than a dozen runners—sometimes not so many as that. Each entrant puts up the sum of £4, and the total sum is the prize won by the **second** competitor to reach the post. The outright winner must content himself (or herself) with the interest on a sum bequeathed by Lord Burlington and associates in 1618, which amounts these days to a bare £6; the runner-up/winner's prize may be nearer to £50! But such is the spirit engendered among competitors in this farcical-seeming horse race, in which 'no rider that layeth hold on, or striketh, another rider shall receive any prize whatsover', that competition for first place rather than second is every bit as keen as it would be at Epsom, Kentucky or Longchamps. A jockey much prefers the modest monetary award and the glory of having beaten his rivals, to the more substantial monetary prize and the relative ignomiry of having been beaten at the post.

An interesting sidelight on the story of the Kiplingcotes Derby is to be found in the fact that, some years ago, there were for once no entrants at all. The traditional race was in jeopardy, for the course **must** be kept open by an annual race. A horse was therefore walked over it between the hours of noon and 1 o'clock on the third Thursday of the month and methodically paraded through all the adjacent parishes; this prevented the breaking of a four-and-a-half-centuries-old tradition.

SWORD-DANCING

Sword-dancing is a spectacular variant of morris dancing. Though of the same basic ritual it belongs primarily to the North Country. It may be witnessed in Lincolnshire, possibly linked with the Revesby Plough Mummers' Play, but it thrives best between the North Riding and the border of Northumbria with Scotland. It has no set occasion, but is to be witnessed at its best during the summer months, at places such as Grenoside and North Skelton, Handsworth and Flamborough. It does not demand great perspicuity to deduce that the action witnessed is a mimed version of a ceremony that has a very remote origin indeed—as ancient as any in the calendar.

Unlike the morris dancers, the eight (or sometimes only five) men flourish not handkerchiefs (or deer antlers) but swords. These are sometimes a yard long and will be of steel or supple, willowy wood. This is essential, for the climax of the dancing is the lock': an intricate interweaving of the swords so that they can be held aloft by one hilt. It is this framework of steel or wood that will be used either in the mock ceremony of the mirror-framing or in the more sinister ritual of decapitating the sacrificial victim. This climactic moment is built up by the increasingly elaborate and strenuous dancing. Starting with a procession, it ends with the forming of a close ring, during which the 'lock' is constructed.

The dancers ordinarily wear white trousers, or breeches, often topped by a semi-military tunic, and a variety of headgear. They will be led by a King, or Captain, and may be accompanied by a number of traditional figures, many of whom belong to the traditional Mummers' plays. These may include the Fool, Besom Betsy, Pickle Herring, All-Spice, and the Quack, also known as the Ten-pound Doctor. The climax is the ceremonial decapitation. The Fool, or sometimes the King himself, has the lock of swords dropped about his neck as he kneels before the dancers. This is the death of the Old Year. When he rises—re-born by the ministrations of the doctor and midwife Besty—the return of life has been symbolised. The theme of resurrection, whether of man, beast or crop, is shown by this, and by many similar traditional customs, to date infinitely further back than merely the Christian era.

RIPON HORN BLOWER

The focal point of this ancient market town, with a population of about 10,000 and a small but most unusual fifteenth-century cathedral, is the spacious market place. On its high market cross the weather-vane takes the form of the Wakeman's House itself. At exactly 9 o'clock each evening the Wakeman or, as he was later referred to, the Mayor's Hornblower, emerges from the house to perform a ritual act that is known to have been carried out for at least 500 years and is traditionally believed to have been inaugurated in the days of King Alfred, 500 years earlier still. For centuries the Wakeman was Ripon's fiirst citizen; in 1604 he was appointed mayor.

He wears a livery consisting of a fawn three-quarter-length buttoned tunic-coat, gloves and a tricorne, and carries, slung across his chest by a leather strap, the Ripon Millenary Horn. Now 100 years old, it has replaced the very ancient Charter Horn, believed to be of Saxon origin and still to be seen, bearing the emblems of successive Wakemen from AD886. The new horn is a beautifully proportioned semi-circle of buffalo horn more than 2ft in diameter, with silver mountings. Putting it to his practised lips, the Wakeman blows a long, undulating blast upon it, a blast repeated at each corner, and finally outside the town hall overlooking the market place. Inscribed across its facade above the supporting pillars is the city's motto: EXCEPT YE LORD KEEP YE CITTIE YE WAKEMAN WAKETH IN VAIN. It is an interesting fact that this motto has been adopted by the town of Ripon, Wisconsin, USA.

The sentiment is a pious one. But in fact the true origin of today's picturesque ceremony lies in the establishment, many centuries ago, of a patrol service organised by the Wakeman and paid for in the form of a modest toll by citizens with a regard for the safety of their property: an insurance against burglary and fire. It was identified with the curfew —the 'couvre-feu' which, in the Middle Ages, when almost all buildings were of highly inflammable timber, ordered citizens to dowse their fires. If a burglary was committed during the hours of darkness it was the Wakeman who had to compensate the insured citizen for his losses.

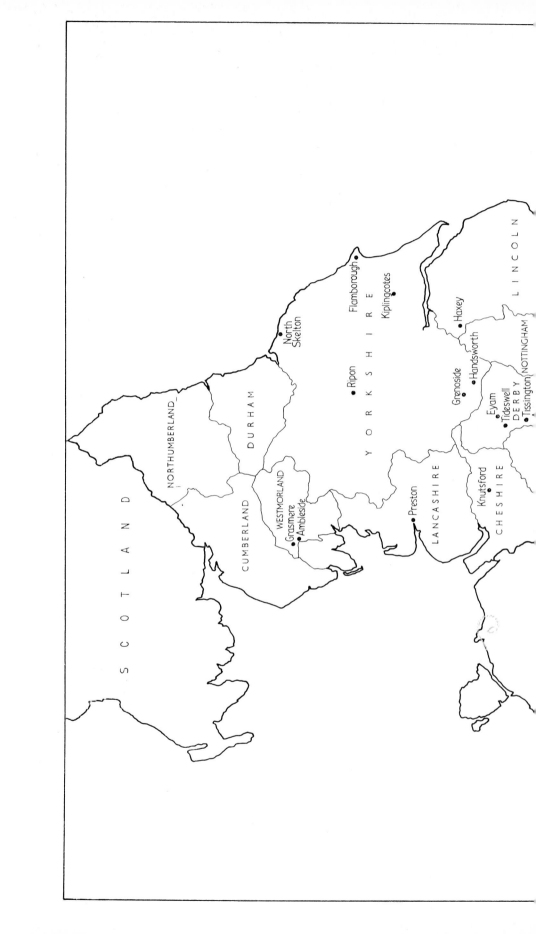

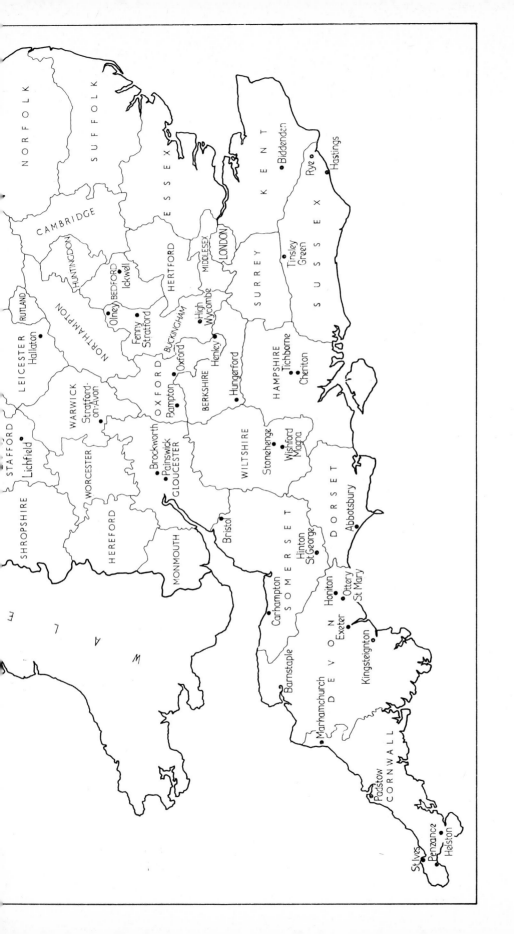

SOME ADDITIONAL CUSTOMS AND TRADITIONS

Barely fifty out of the very considerable number of customs and traditions that, happily, still survive in England (Scottish and Welsh examples have no place here, for they deserve a book to themselves) have been described in detail, and illustrated, in the foregoing pages. Of those that have not been dealt with, almost every one is as deserving of inclusion in the body of this book as are those that do appear there. Selection has been difficult, and the result will undoutedly seem invidious—especially to readers living in the localities where these occasions are still held and who thus look in vain for what they quite justifiably consider merit more detailed mention.

Within the space available, however, drastic pruning of the flourishing tree of custom and tradition had to be undertaken. So, as some compensation to those who have inevitably been disappointed in this regard, there now follow a hundred and more customs and traditions that were, so to speak, runners-up in the contest for inclusion. They are listed, like the others, under the counties in which they are to be found; but they are, inevitably, listed only very briefly indeed. Details about them can of course be filled in by reference to the books which are mentioned, by author, title, publisher and date, in the Bibliography that follows the list.

Bedfordshire: May Day ceremonies and the crowning of the May Queen at Elstow. Orange-rolling at Pascombe Pit, Dunstable Downs, Good Friday. Wilkes Charity Perambulation at Leighton Buzzard, Rogation Monday.

Berkshire: Candle Auction at Aldermaston, 13 December (triennially). Bread Dole at Ufton, mid-lent. Mayor of Ock Street election at Abingdon, mid-June. Maids' Money ceremony at Reading, Good Friday. Morris dancing at Abingdon, late June. Bun-throwing at Abingdon, in November.

Cheshire: Bawming the Thorn at Appleton, mid-July. Miracle Plays Festival at Chester, early July. Soulcaking at Comberbach, All Souls' Day. Soulcaking at Antrobus, All Souls' Day.

Cornwall: Hurling the Silver Ball at St Ives, early February. Hurling the Silver Ball at St Columb Major/Minor, early February. Banishing the Witches at St Cleer, Midsummer Eve. Knill Steeple dancing near St Ives, late July (quinquennially). Ancient Gorsedds (Bards festivals) at various sites, early September.

Derbyshire: Clipping at Church at Burbage, late July. Padley Martyrs Commemoration at Grindleford, mid-July. Garland Day at Castleton, 29 May.

Devonshire: Ye Fyshinge Feast at Plymouth, summer Saturdays (variable). Ale Tasting and Bread Weighing at Ashburton, late November. Turning the Devil's Boulder at Shebbear, 5 November.

Andrew's Dole at Bideford, 1 January. Beating-the-Clock race at Bideford, early June. Blessing-the-Plough ceremony at Exeter Cathedral, early January. Grand Pony Fair at Princetown, early September. St Giles's Fair at Barnstaple, second half of September.

Co Durham: Shrovetide football at Sedgefield.

Essex: Dunmow Flitch Trial at Gt Dunmow, Whit Monday. Morris dancing at Thaxted, Easter Monday and Whit Monday. Gooseberry Fair at Tollesbury, early July. Oyster Feast celebrations at Colchester, late October.

Gloucestershire: Redcliffe Pipe Walk at Bristol, late October. Boxing Day Mummers etc at Marshfield. Bread-and-Cheese Throwing at St Briavels, Whitsuntide. The Water Game at Bourton-on-the-Water, late August. St Anne's Well Pilgrimage at Bristol, late July. Cranham Feast at Cranham, mid-August Monday. Scuttlebrook Wake at Chipping Campden, Saturday after Whitsuntide.

Hampshire: Christmas Mummers at Overton. Mumming Play at Crookham, Boxing Day. Court of the Verderers at Lyndhurst, mid-January (quinquennially). Knighthood of Southampton Old Green Championship, early August.

Herefordshire: Pax Cake distribution at King's Capel, Easter. Pax Cake distribution at Hentland, Easter.

Huntingdonshire: Dicing for New Bibles at St Ives, Whit Tuesday. Ancient Fair at St Ives, Whit Monday.

Kent: Tilting the Quintain at Offham, May Day. Jossing Block Money at Ightham, mid-Lent. Blessing the cherry orchards at Newington, Rogation Sunday. Blessing the sea at Margate, July. Blessing the sea at Folkestone, July. Blessing the sea at Whitstable, August. The Admiralty Court on the Medway at Rochester, early July. Blessing the oyster-bed waters at Whitstable, late August. Guy Fawkes celebrations at Edenbridge, 5 November.

Lancashire: Walking Day at Salford; ditto at Manchester; ditto at Warrington, late June/earliest July. Pageant of the Black Knight at Ashton-under-Lyne, late September.

Leicestershire: Beating the Bounds at Leicester, Rogationtide (triennally). Candle Auction at Grimston, late December. Selling the Wether at Enderby, Whit Monday.

Lincolnshire: Flower Parade at Spalding, a Saturday in May or June according to the weather. Candle Auction at Old Bolingbroke, late December. The Mumming Play at Revesby, Plough Monday.

London: The Pancake Greaze at Westminster School, Shrove Tuesday. Beating the Bounds at St Clement Danes, Rogation Week. Beating the Bounds at the Tower, Rogation Week (triennially). Blessing the Throats in Ely Place, Holborn, 3 February.

Norfolk: The Ancient Mart at King's Lynn, mid-February. Pilgrimage to the Shrine of Our Lady of Walsingham, Whit Monday.

Northumberland: Shrovetide Football at Alnwick. Bumping the Freeholders at Newbiggin-by-the-Sea mid-May. Salmon-net blessing at Norham-on-Tweed, mid-February.

Nottinghamshire: Cradle-rocking ceremony at Blidworth, early February. Goose Fair at Nottingham, Michaelmas.

Oxfordshire: The Great Shirt Race at Bampton, Easter Monday. St Giles Fair at Oxford, early September.

Somerset: Gunpowder Plot celebrations at Bridgwater, at Glastonbury, at Highbridge, and at Wells, 5 November. Candle Auction at Tatworth, early April. Egg Shackling at Shepton Beauchamp, and at Stoke St Gregory, Shrovetide. Beating the Bounds at Cannington, Rogationtide. Hobby-Horse Festival at Minehead, May Day.

Staffordshire: Riding the City Bounds at Lichfield, early September.

Suffolk: The Cake & Ale ceremony at Bury St Edmunds, early January.

Surrey: Dicing for the Maids' Money at Guildford, January. Forty Shillings Day at Wootton, mid-February.

Sussex: Blessing the plough at Chichester, mid-January. Good Friday Skipping at Alciston. Blessing the sea at Hastings, late May. Gunpowder Plot celebrations at Lewes, 5 November.

Warwickshire: Wardmote at Meriden, early August. Mop Fair at Warwick, October. May Day Revels at Welford-on-Avon. Wroth Silver Money ceremony on Knightlow Hill, early November.

Wiltshire: Christmas Eve Mummers at Andover.

Yorkshire: The Antient Silver Arrow contest at Scorton, August. Pace Egging and Mumming Play at Midgley, Easter. Gawthorpe May Festival at Ossett, early May. The Penny Hedge ceremony at Whitby, Ascension Eve. Maypole dancing at Wadsworth, May Day. The Burning of Bartle at West Witton, August. Blessing the sea at Whitby, May. Waits on the Moors at Pickering, Christmas week. Pancake race on Whitby Pier, Shrove Tuesday. Miracle Plays Festival and Arts Festival at York, summer (triennially). Raising of the (tallest-by-tradition) Maypole at Barwick-in-Elmet, Whit Tuesday (triennially). Perambulating the Bounds at Richmond, Rogationtide.

BIBLIOGRAPHY

The number of books that have been written about England's customs and traditions is legion. Many of them are extremely erudite; others quite superficial. From all of them, however, something worth-while may be gleaned. In addition to the full-length books there are of course innumerable monographs and learned papers, of interest primarily to the student and the specialist, perhaps in regard to one particular type of custom, or to one particular area of the country. To list even a fraction of the material available would demand more space than can be found in a compilation such as this. The two dozen or so titles that follow are no more than a bare selection, making no claim to being comprehensive. Some of them also contain bibliographies; these will be of interest and value to those readers who wish to pursue a virtually inexhaustible subject at least as far as its nearer horizons.

Addison, W.	*English Fairs and Markets*	(Batsford, 1953)
Bett, H.	*English Myths and Traditions*	(Batsford, 1952)
Brand, J.	*Popular Antiquities of Great Britain* (2 vols)	(Rivington, 1905)
Brasch, R.	*How Did It Begin? Customs and Superstitions and Their Romantic Origins*	(Longmans, 1965)
Chambers, R.	*The Book of Days* (2 vols)	(Chambers, 1888)
Chaundler, C.	*Everyman's Book of Ancient Customs*	(Mowbray, 1968)
Christian, R.	*Country Life Book of Old English Customs*	(Country Life, 1966)
Ditchfield, P. H.	*Old English Customs*	(Redway, 1896)
Gascoigne, M.	*Discovering English Customs and Traditions*	(Shire Publications, 1969)
Hole, C.	*English Custom and Usage*	(Batsford, 1950)
Hole, C.	*English Sports and Pastimes*	(Batsford, 1949)
Hone, W.	*Every-Day Book*	(Teggy, 1838)
Howard, A.	*Endless Cavalcade*	(Barker, 1964)
Hull, E.	*Folklore of the British Isles*	(Methuen, 1928)
Hunt, C.	*British Customs and Traditions*	(Benn, 1954)
Krythe, M. R.	*All About Myths*	(Harper & Row, 1966)
Pine, L. G.	*Traditions and Customs in Modern Britain*	(Whiting & Wheaton, 1967)
Smith, D. and Newton D.	*British Customs and Festivals*	(Blackie, 1969)
Snell, J. F.	*The Customs of Old England*	(Methuen, 1911)
Spicer, D. G.	*Year Book of English Festivals*	(Wilson, New York, 1954)
Thistleton-Dyer, T.	*British Popular Customs, Past and Present*	(Bell, 1891)
Trent, C.	*BP Book of Festivals and Events in Britain*	(Dent, 1966)
Wagner, L.	*Manners, Customs and Observances*	(Heinemann, 1895)
Walsh, W. S.	*Curiosities of Popular Customs, Rites, Ceremonies, Observancies & Antiquities*	(Lippincott, 1898)
Whistler, L.	*The English Festivals*	(Heinemann, 1947)
Williamson, G. C.	*Curious Survivals, Habits and Customs of The Past that Still Live in the Present*	(Jenkins, 1923)
Wright, A. R.	*British Calendar Customs* (3 vols)	(Glaisher/Folk Lore Society, 1936-40)